Mandala: ritual of Visual *poetry*

Yakman K Tsering

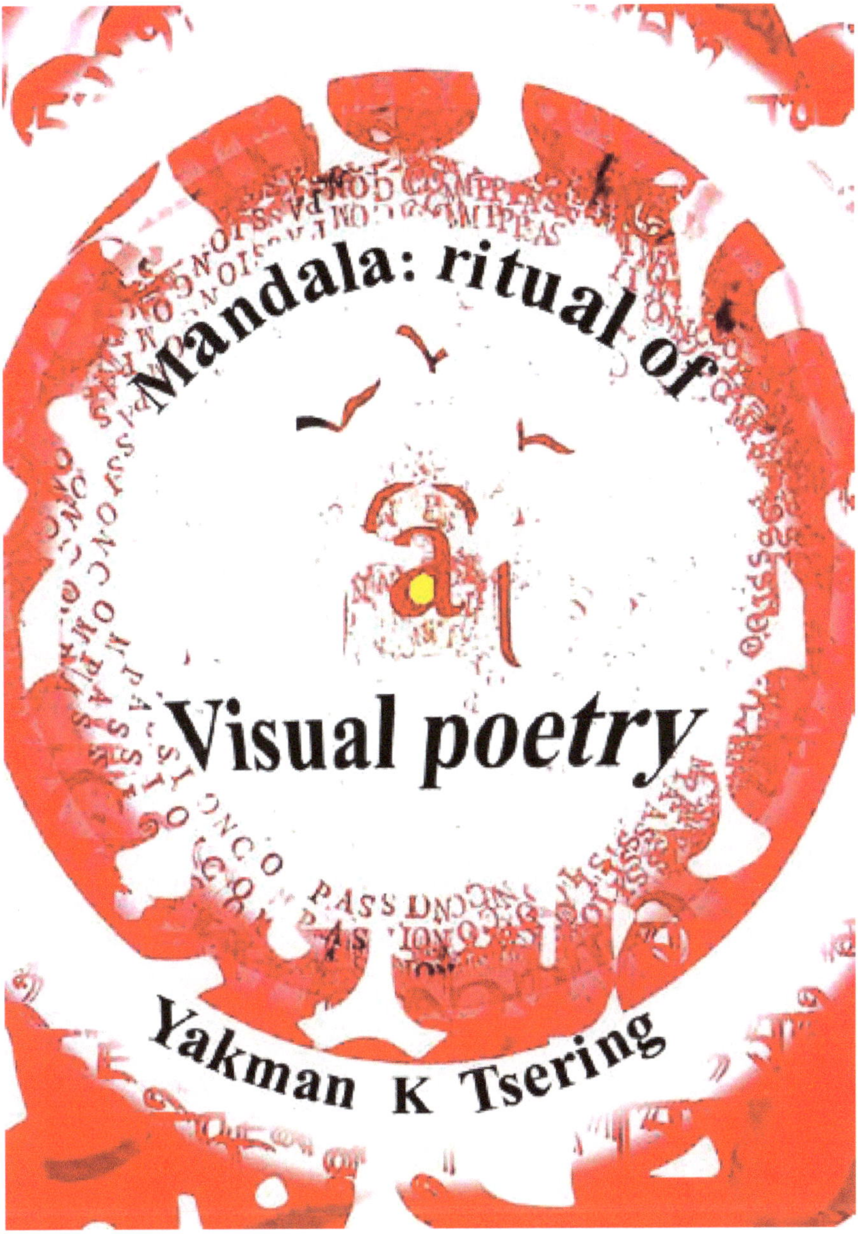

Mandala: ritual of Visual poetry

Yakman K Tsering

Cover Art: compassion by Yakman K Tsering
Cover preparation
by harry k stammer

ISBN: 979-8-9949368-1-8

Sandy Press
Queensland, Australia
&
California, USA

https://sandy-press.com
sandypress2021@gmail.com

Acknowledgements

Some of these visual poems have been published in:
Otoliths, Austria. E. ratio.US. Utsanga, It. We are visual poetry book, Mexico. *Artistonish contemporary art magazine.* Canada. *Goddess arts magazine: issue 6*, Germany. S*ynapse International & Aurapoesiavisal*, Argentina.

My thanks to the respective editors & specially thanks to my friend Karl Kempton

Forward

By Karl Kempton

There are many deep ancestors out of which contemporary visual poetry and visual text art bloomed. From rock art symbols moved to evolve onto portable objects such as pottery, charms and amulets. These patterned objects, wearable and portable, were in wide use in Tibetan culture for hundreds of years before and after conversion to Buddhism out of which came Buddhist prayer flags and prayer wheels. Symbols also migrated onto murals, and mosaics. Perhaps it can be said that the richest development of Tibetan Buddhist expression became the famous and intricate sand mandala paintings now with performances by monks experienced around the world. All these types of symbols and text were and remain highly symbolic and deeply rooted ritual and patterned text from the Shamanistic Bon era.

Out of this rich heritage arrives Yakman K Tsering's *Mandala: ritual of Visual poetry* with its lush, complex at times, delightfully lyrical work resting in and on the pedestal of the mandala form.

Author`s Note

In this book, I explore my thoughts and experiences through visual and experimental poetry. Drawing from daily life, personal history, and global events such as the coronavirus, my work reflects how visual language can heal, communicate, and connect.

By moving between the English letter *A* and the Tibetan letter *Ah*, I examine sound, image, and meaning beyond linguistic boundaries. This book reveals the power of language—visual and symbolic—to express emotion and create global understanding.

This book is an offering of feeling rather than explanation. Through visual and experimental poetry, I hope to communicate something deeply human—how language, in its many forms, can connect us, even when words are not enough.

Mandala: Ritual of Visual Poetry does not ask to be understood in a single direction. It invites you to look slowly, to move intuitively, and to allow meaning to arise on its own. Within these forms, you may encounter reflections of your own emotions, fragments of memory, or moments from your own unfolding life.

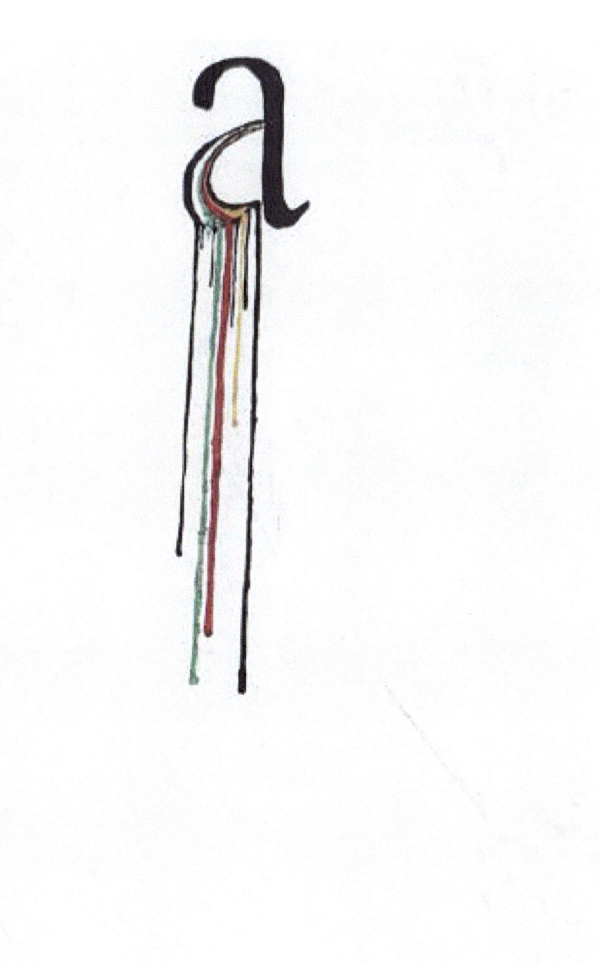

ཨ < a

a > ཨ

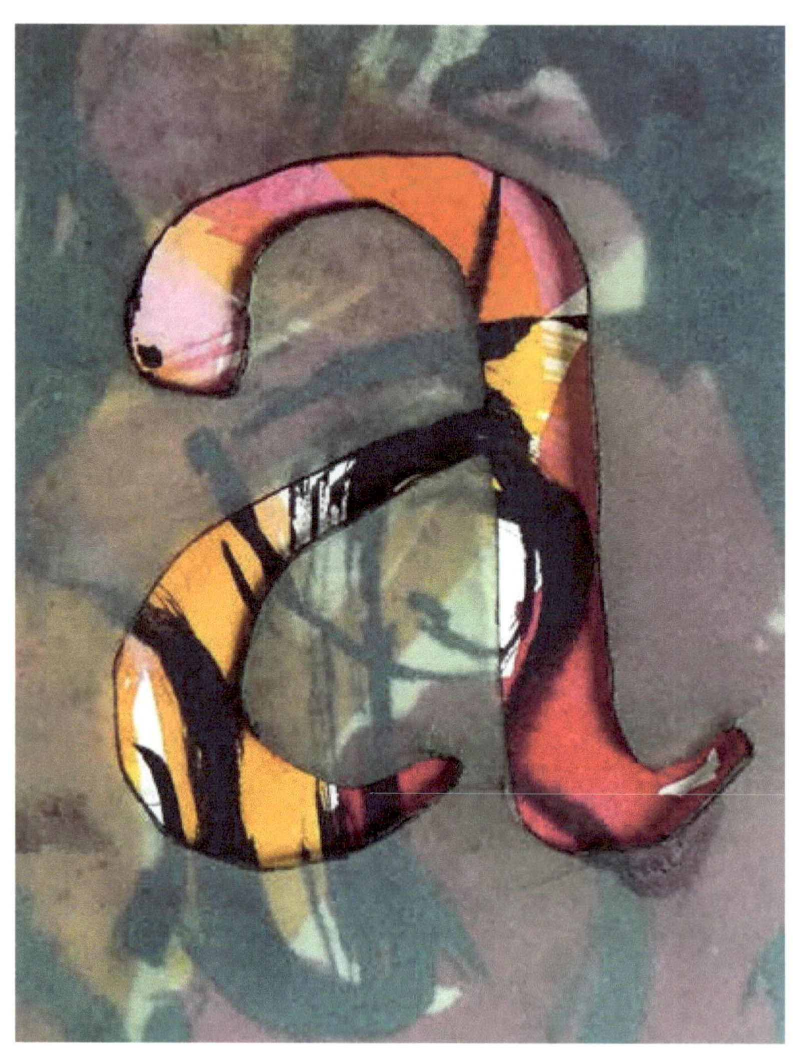

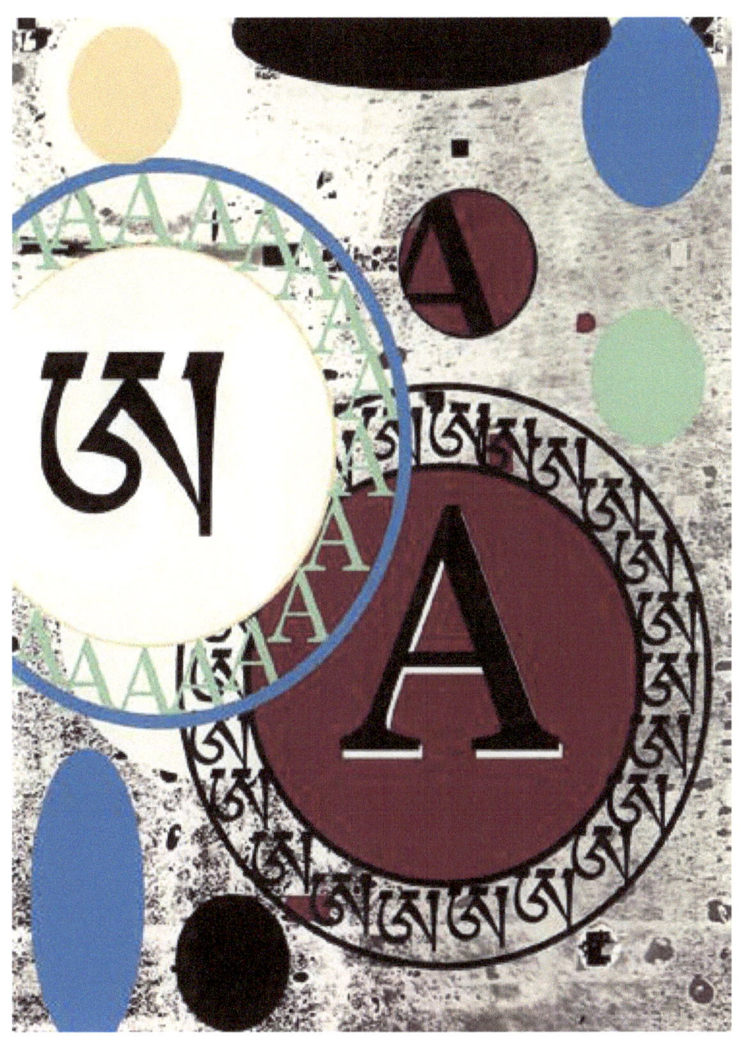

ཨ) a
a (ཨ

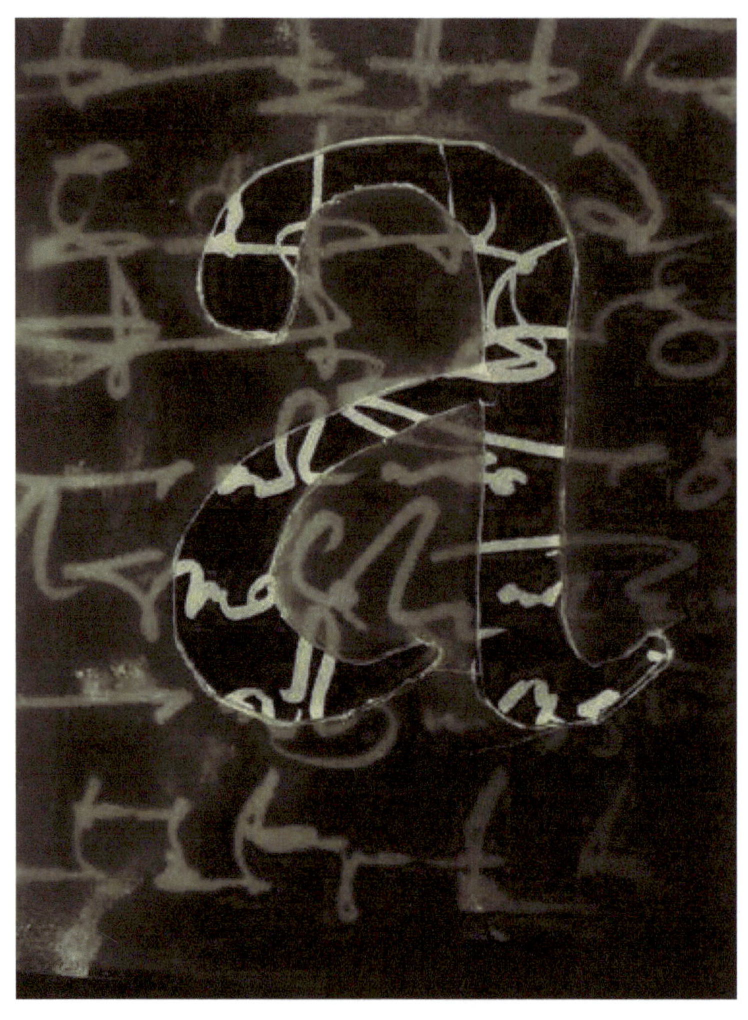

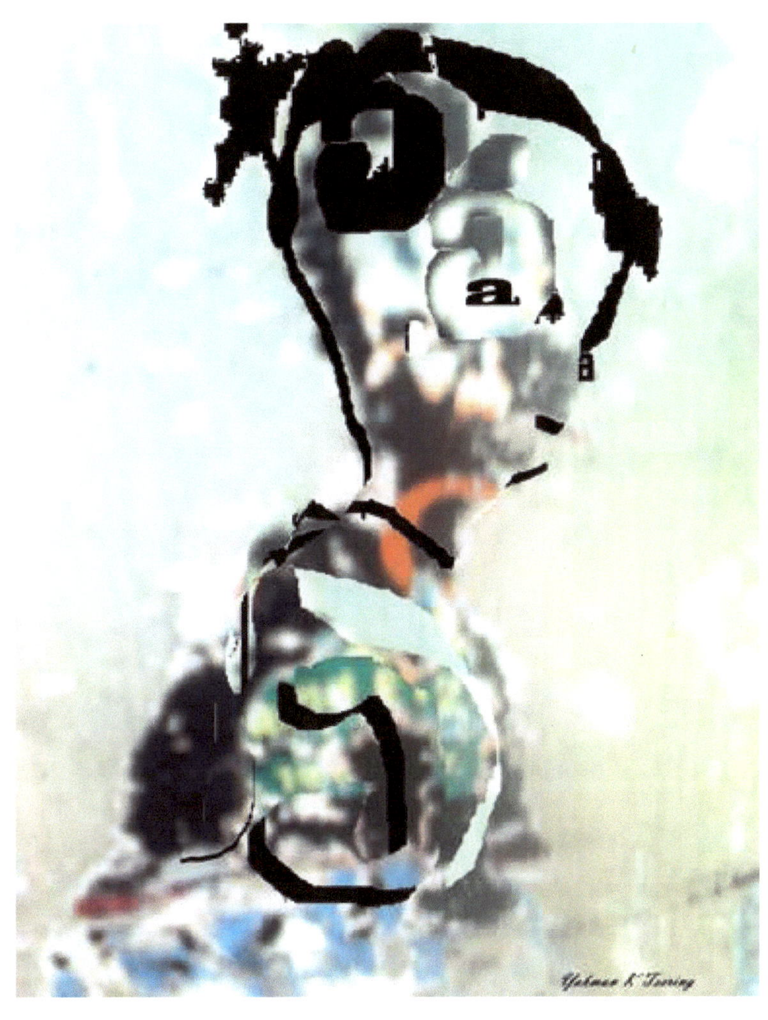

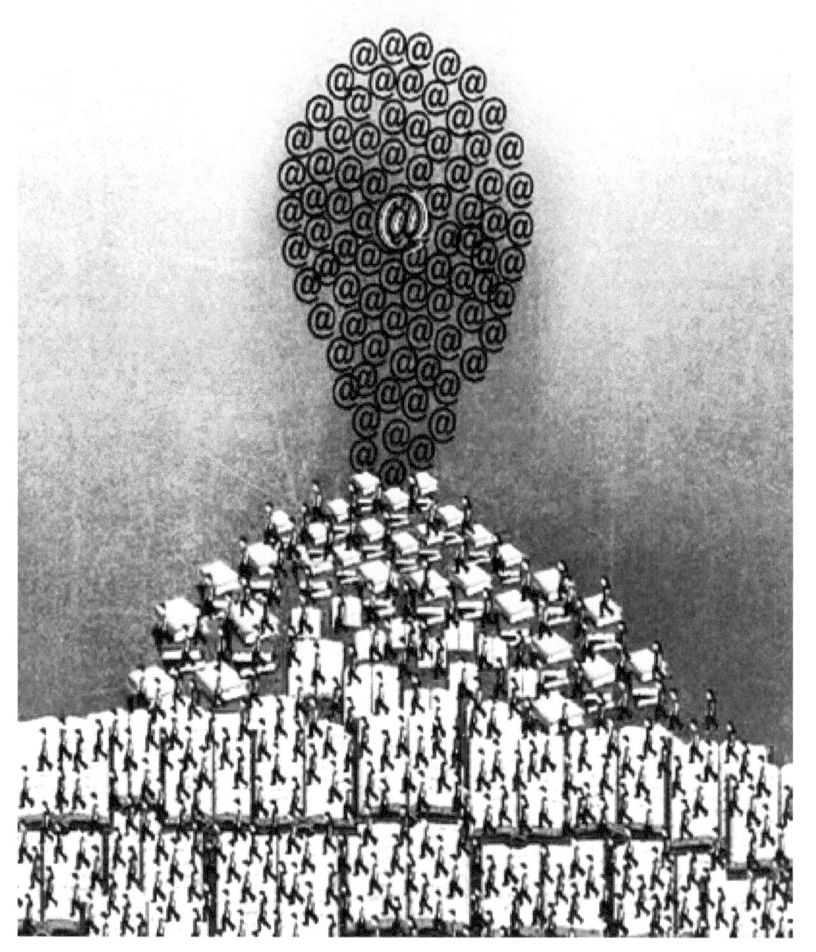

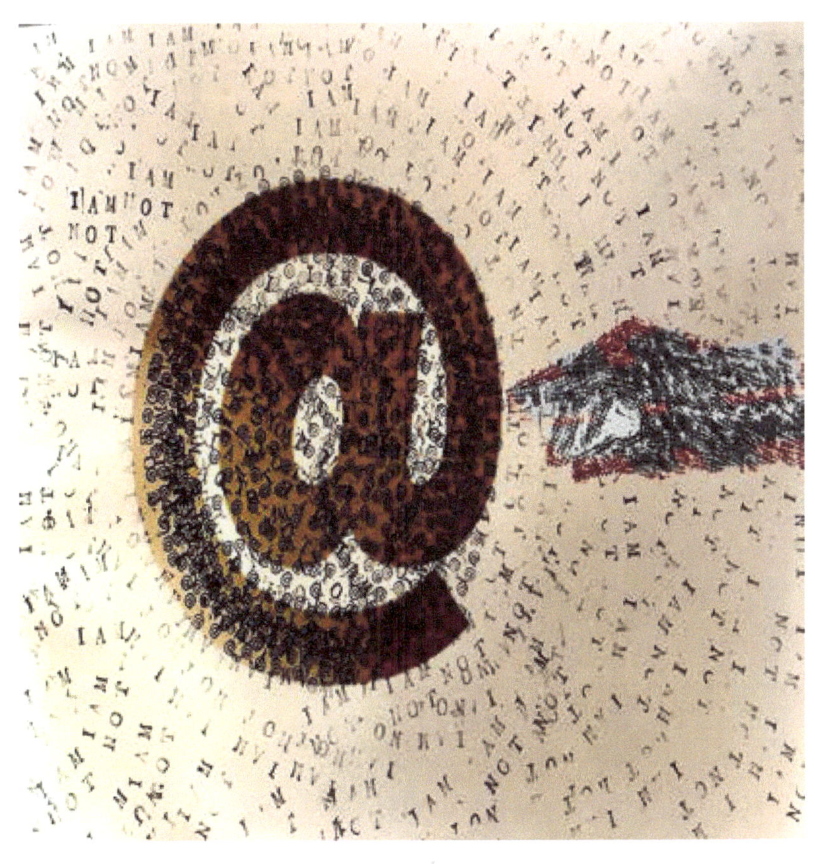
I AM NOT

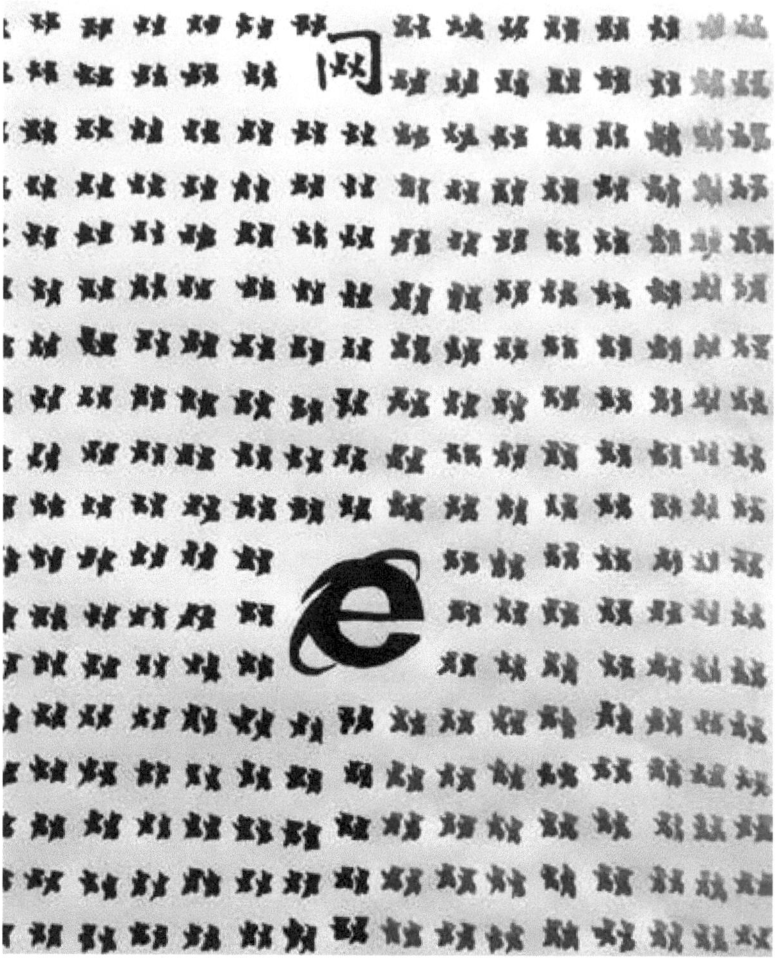

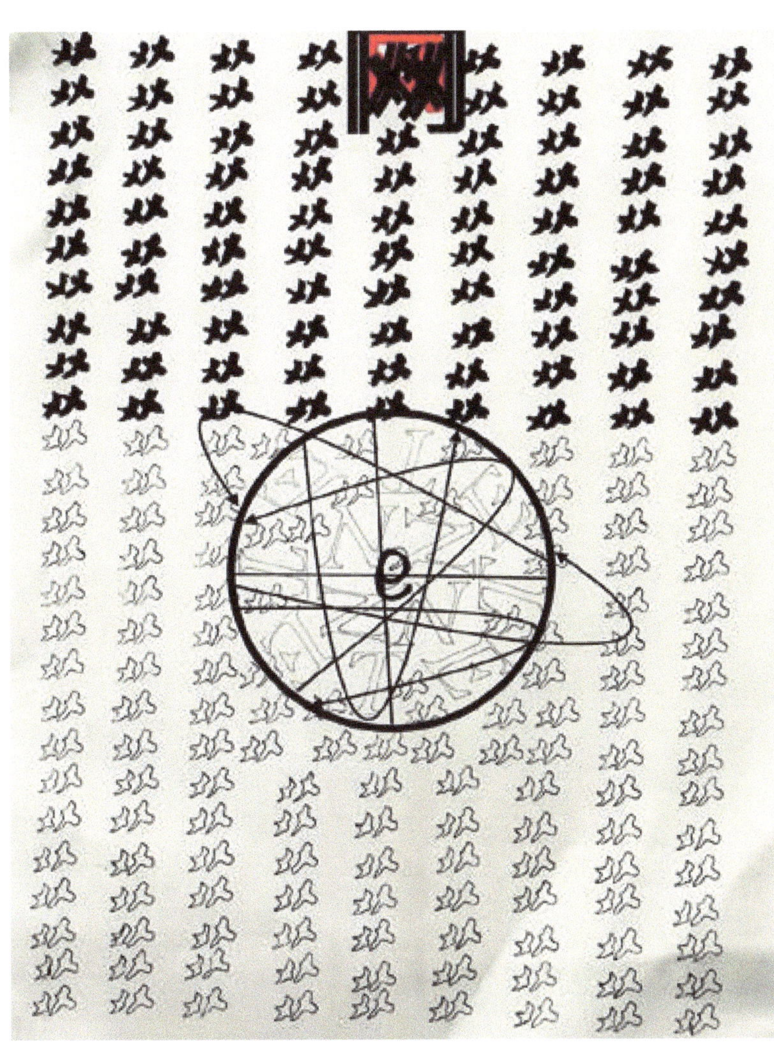

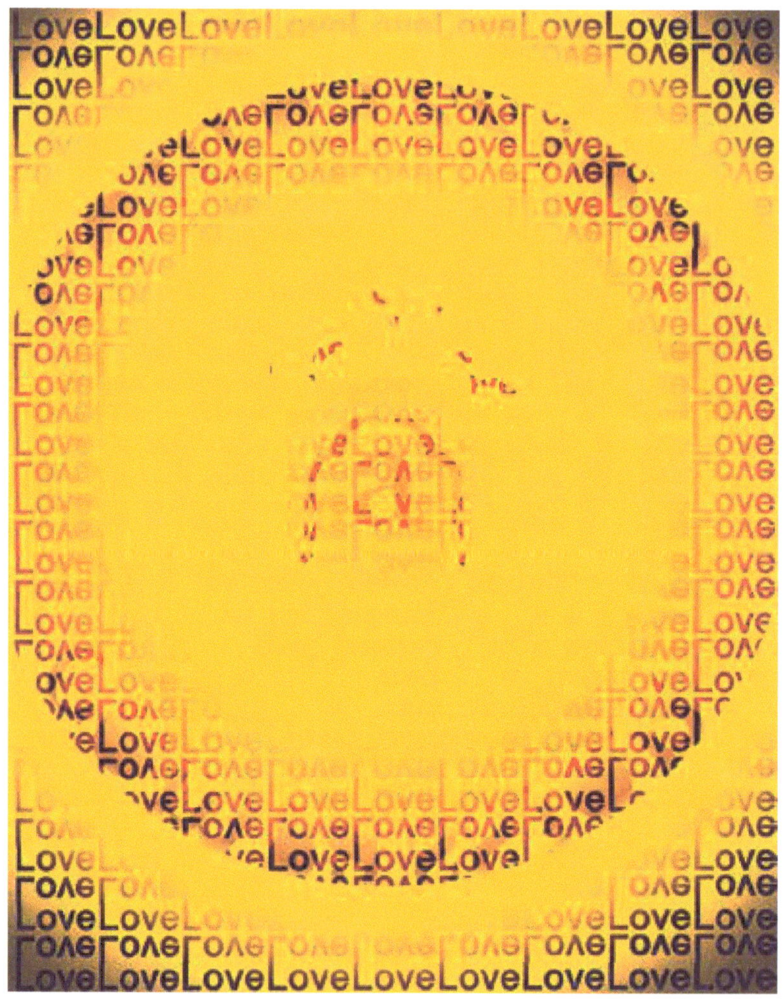

Love

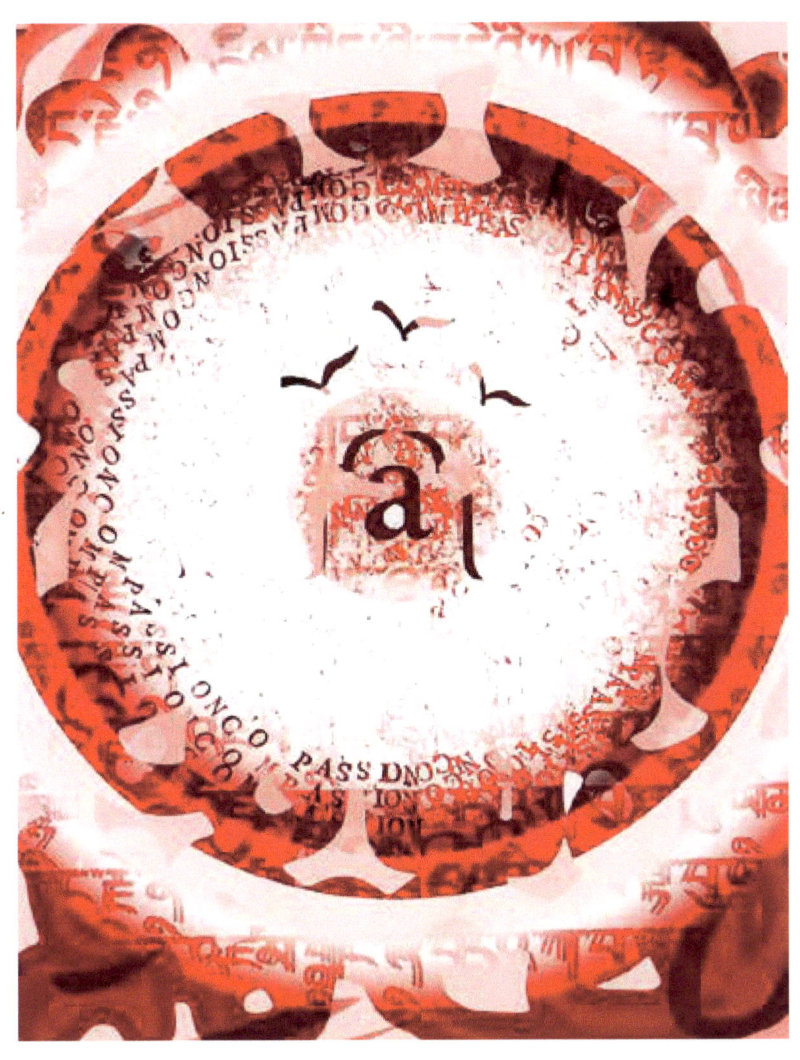

Compassion

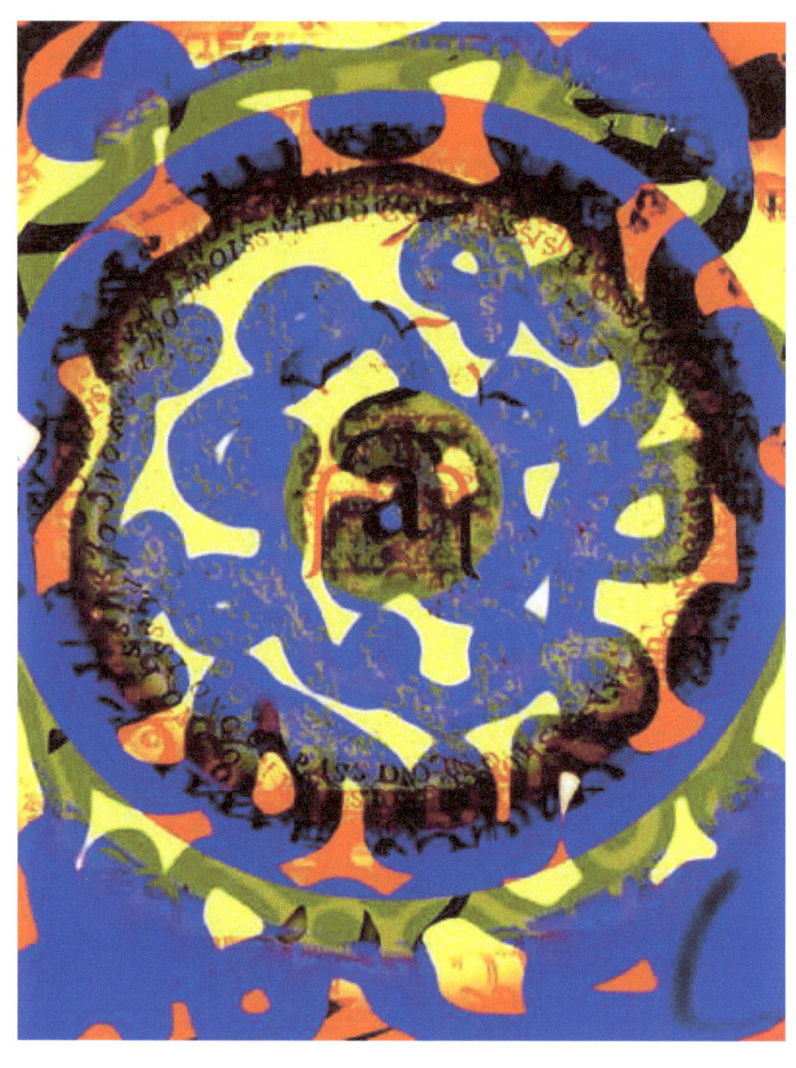

Compassion II

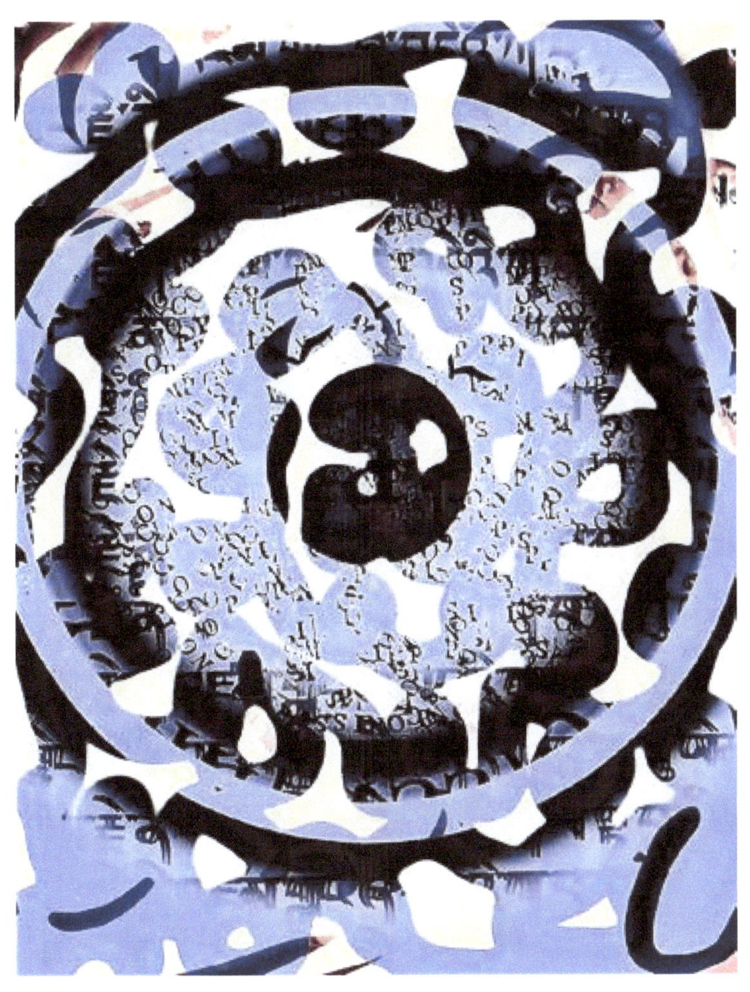

Compassion III

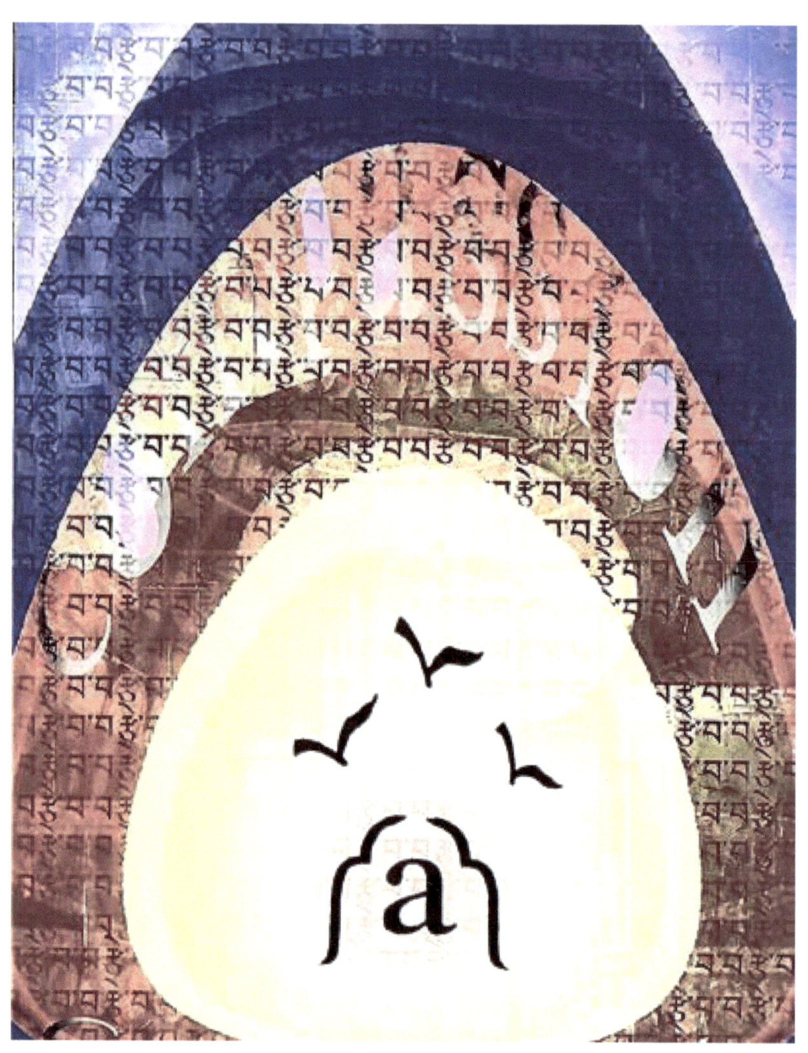

བརྩེ་བ། = Love

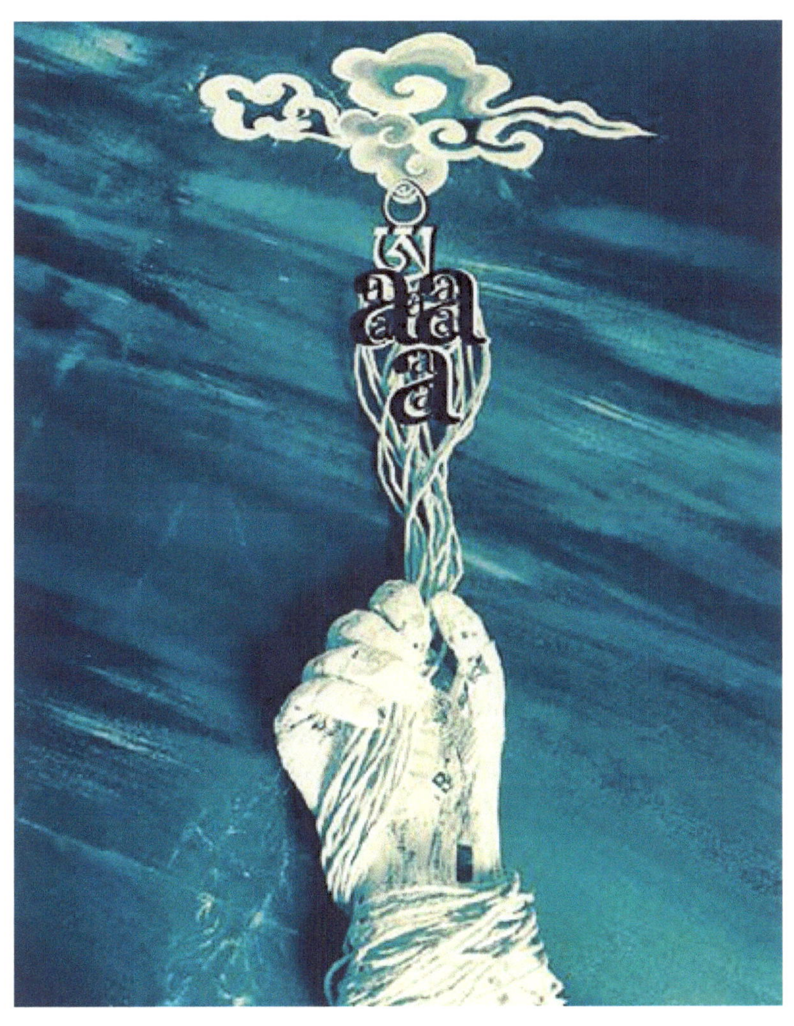

Untitled

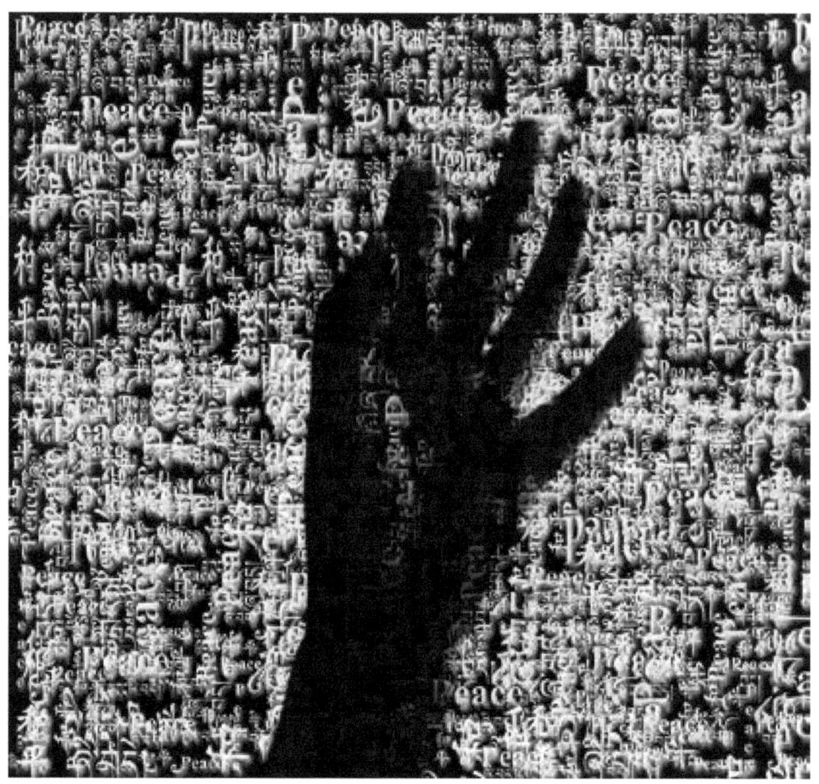

Hand

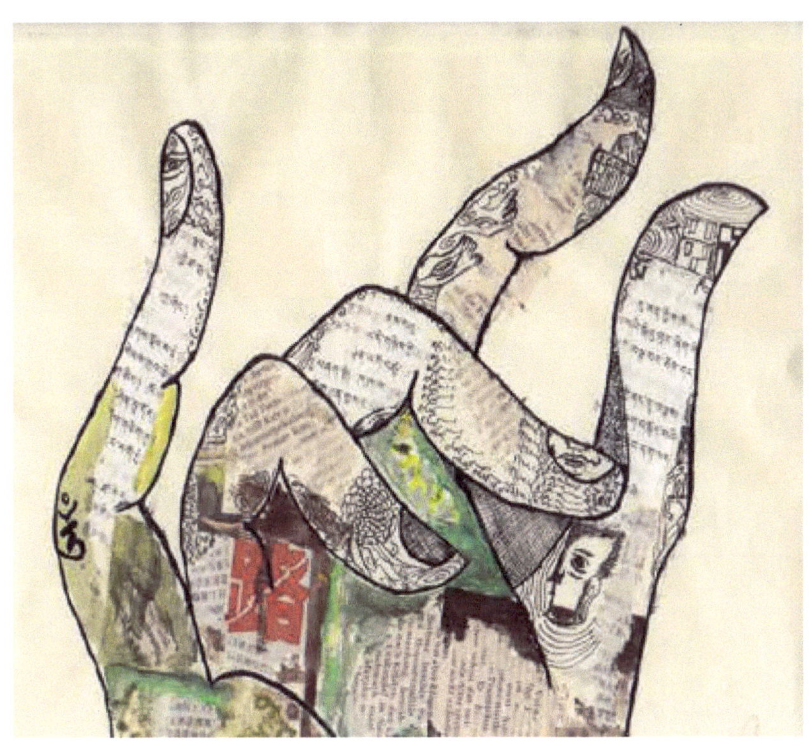

Hand II

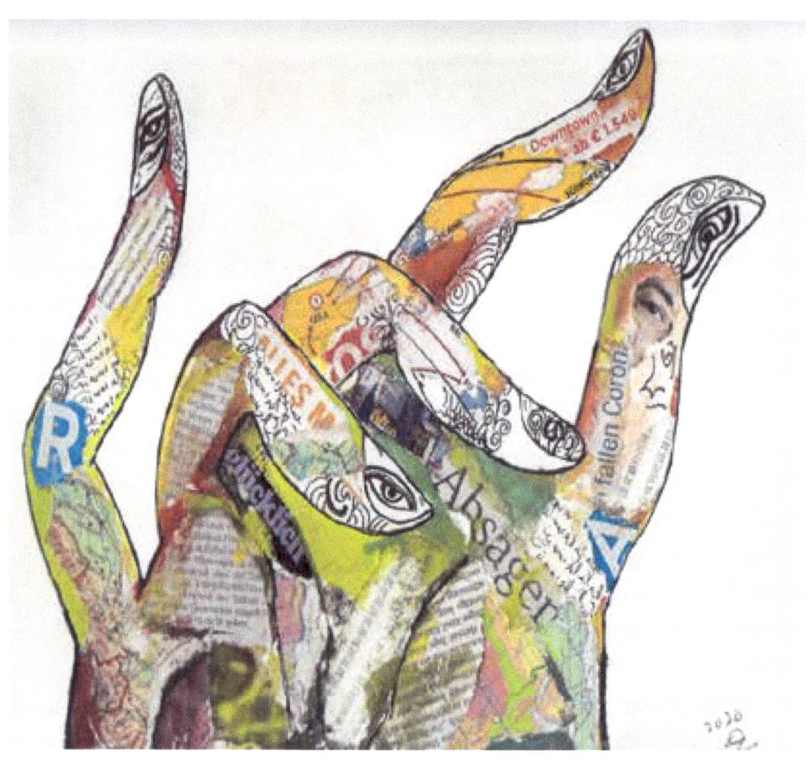

Hand III

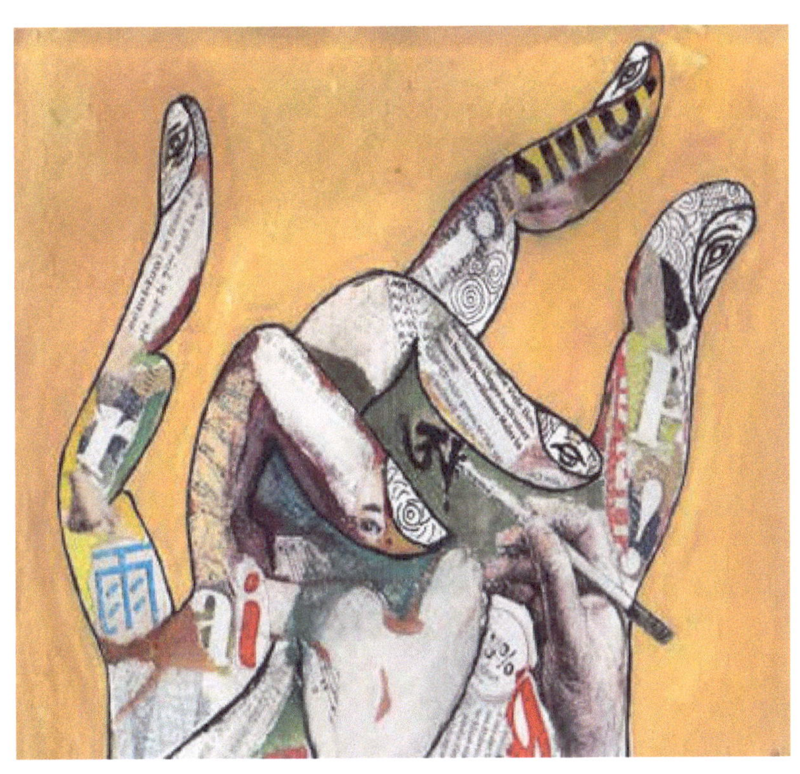

Hand IV

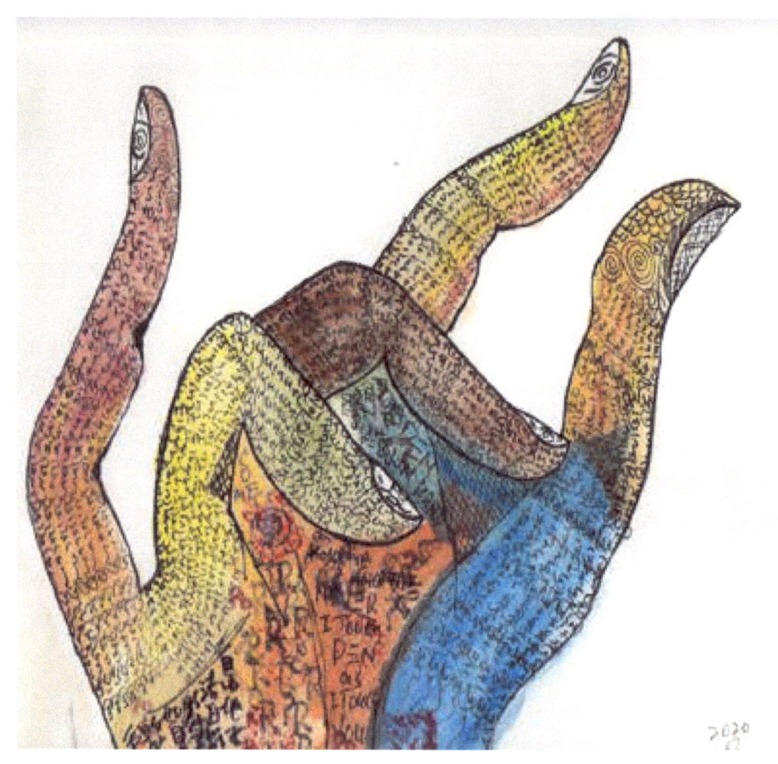

Hand V

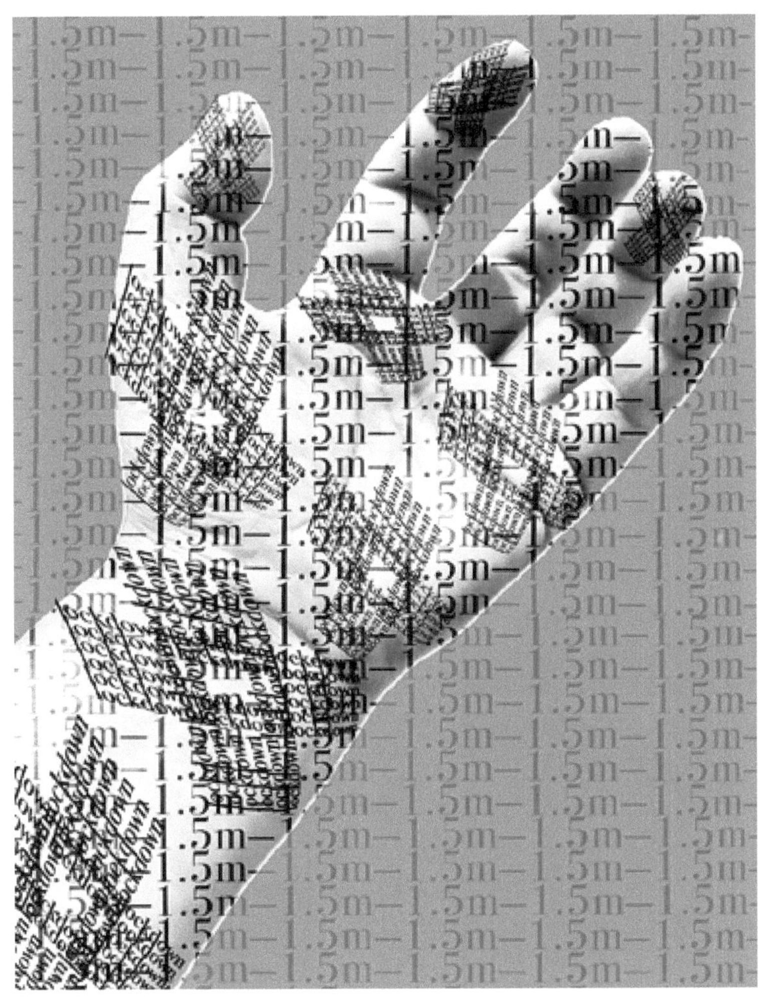

Hand VI

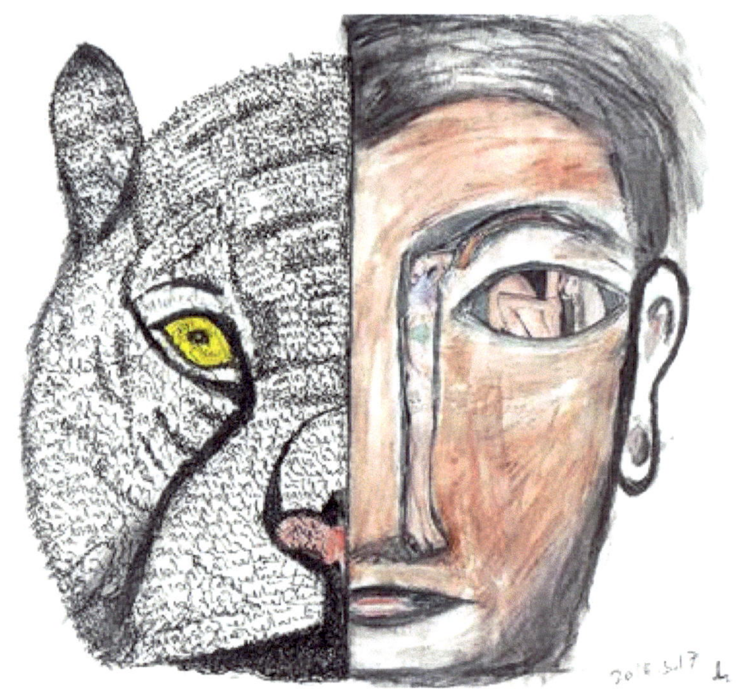

Half face

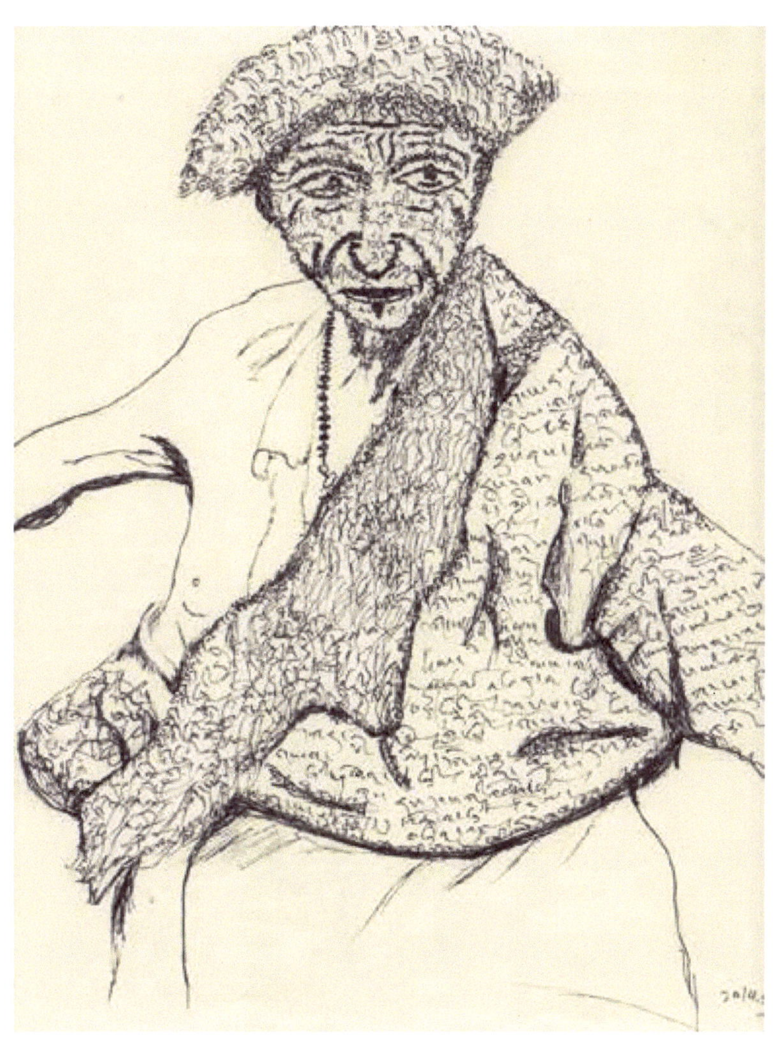

Old Tibetan

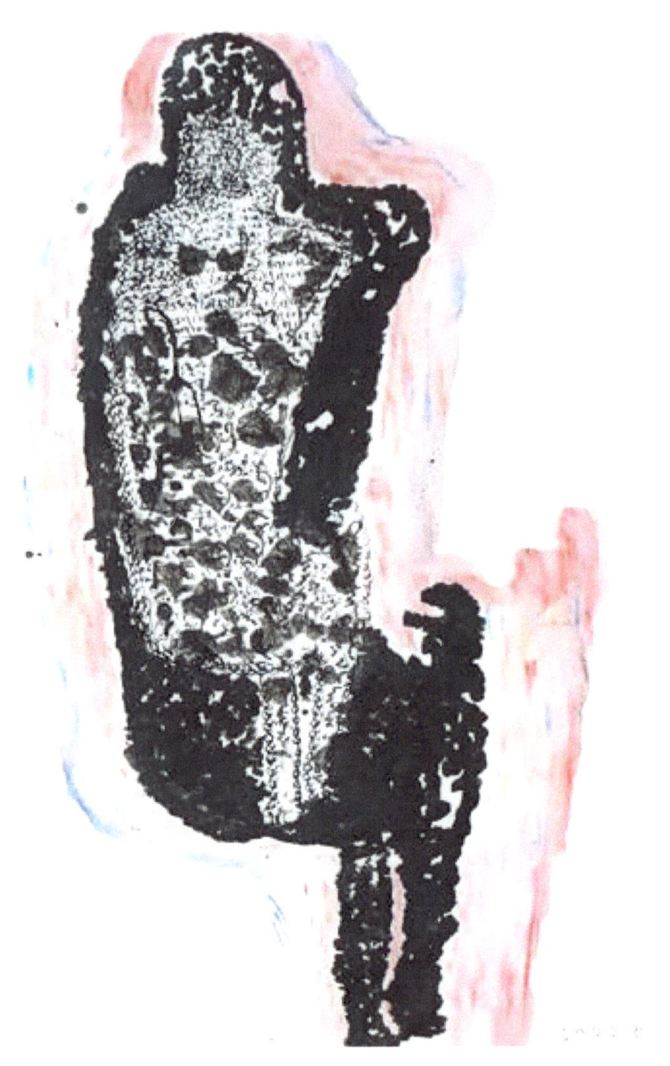

Untitled

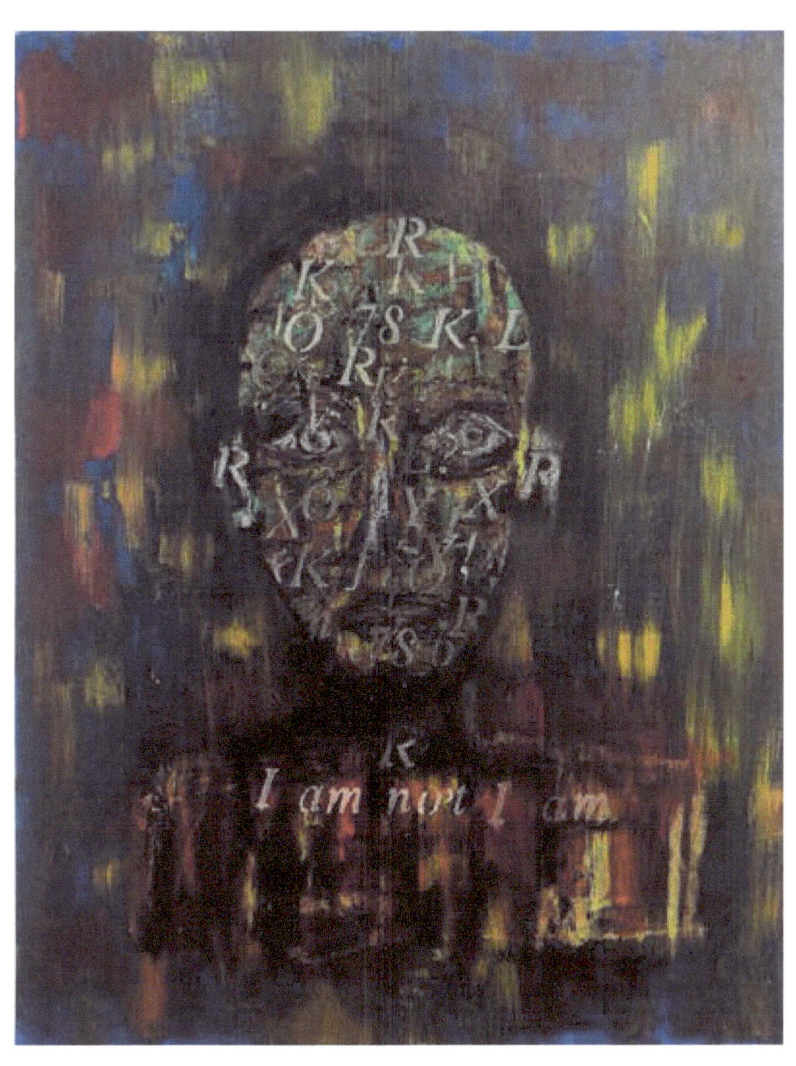

I am not I am
I am not I am
I am not I am

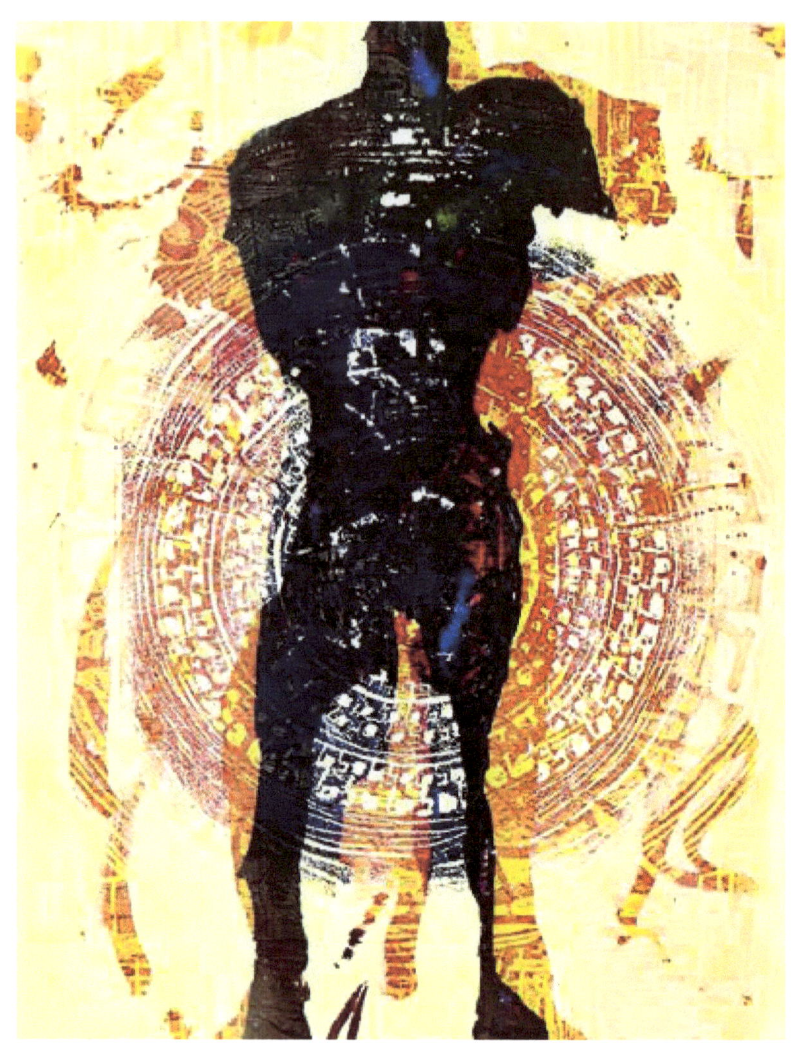

Selflessness

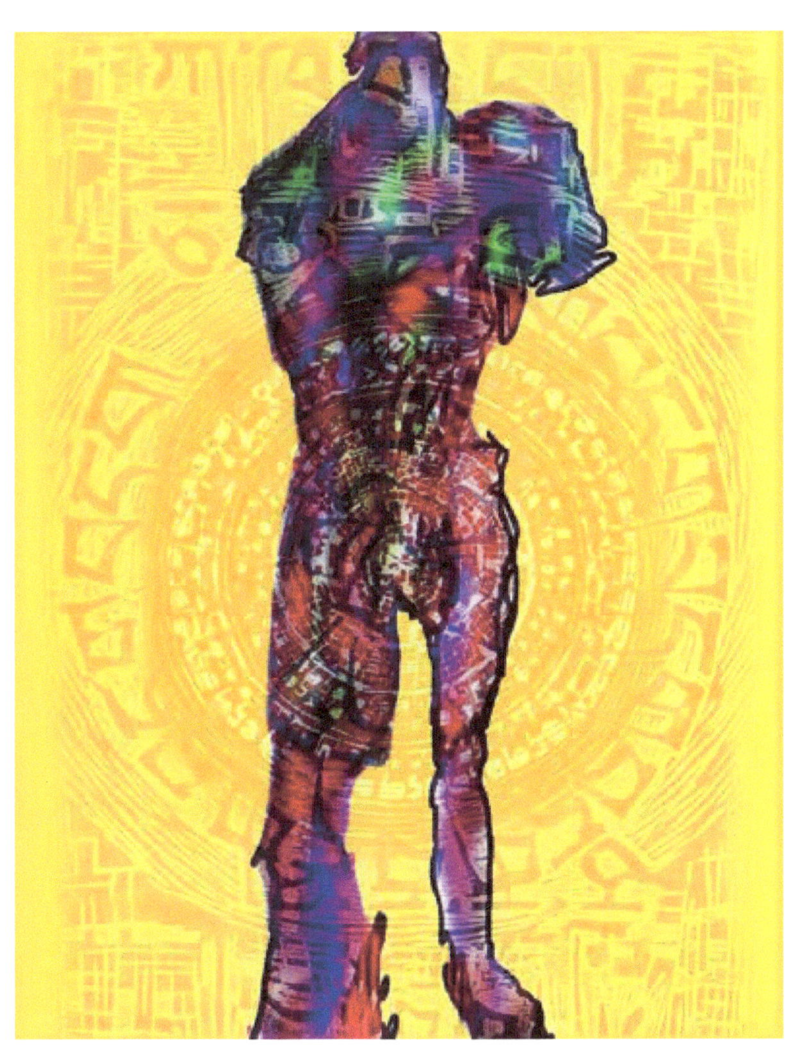

Selflessness II

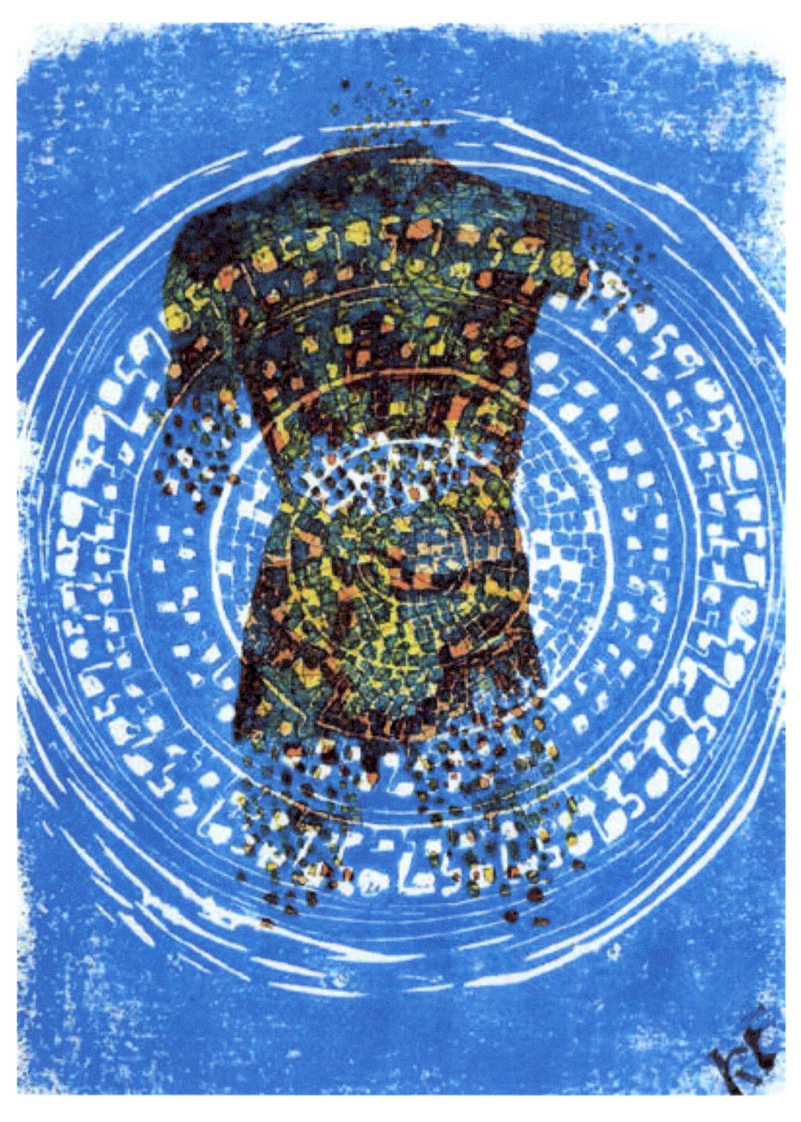

Selflessness III

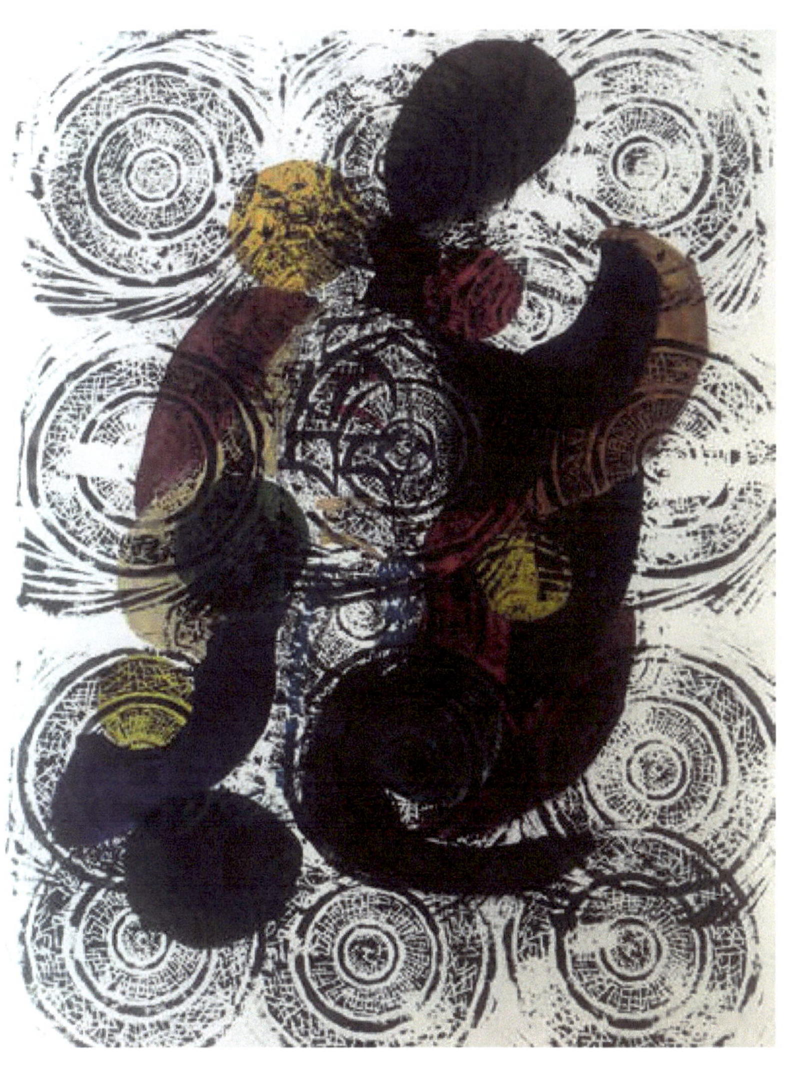

Selflessness IV

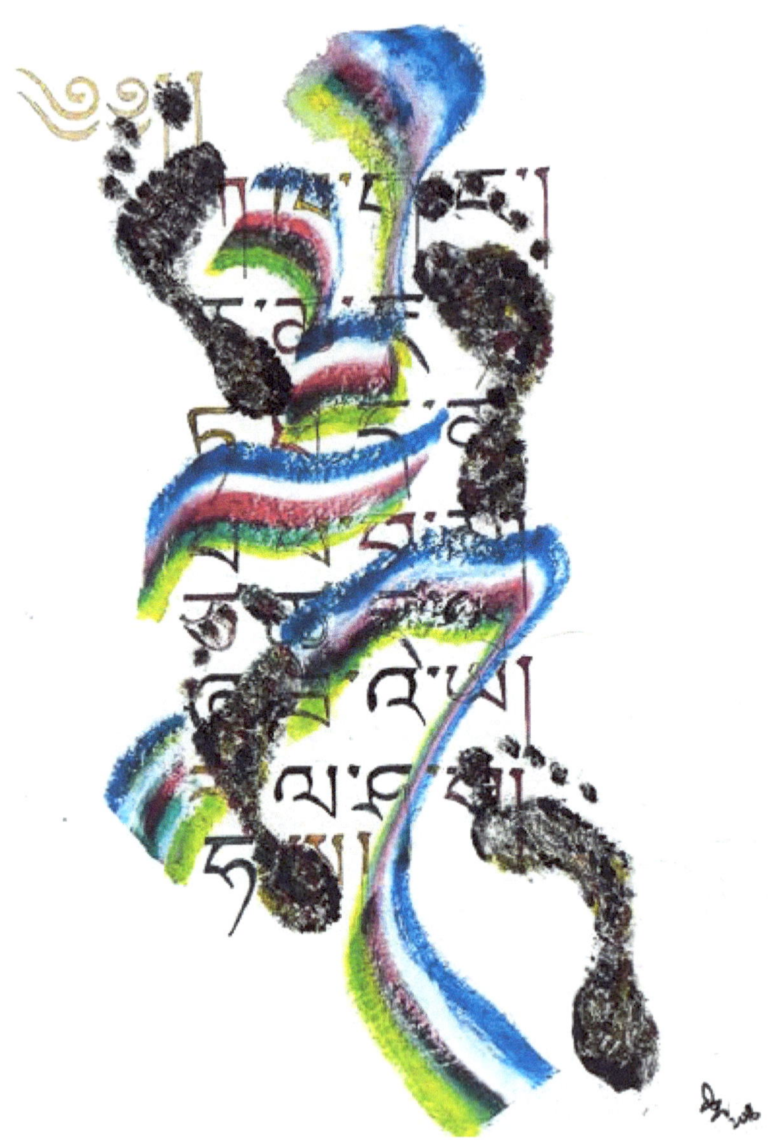

Footprint

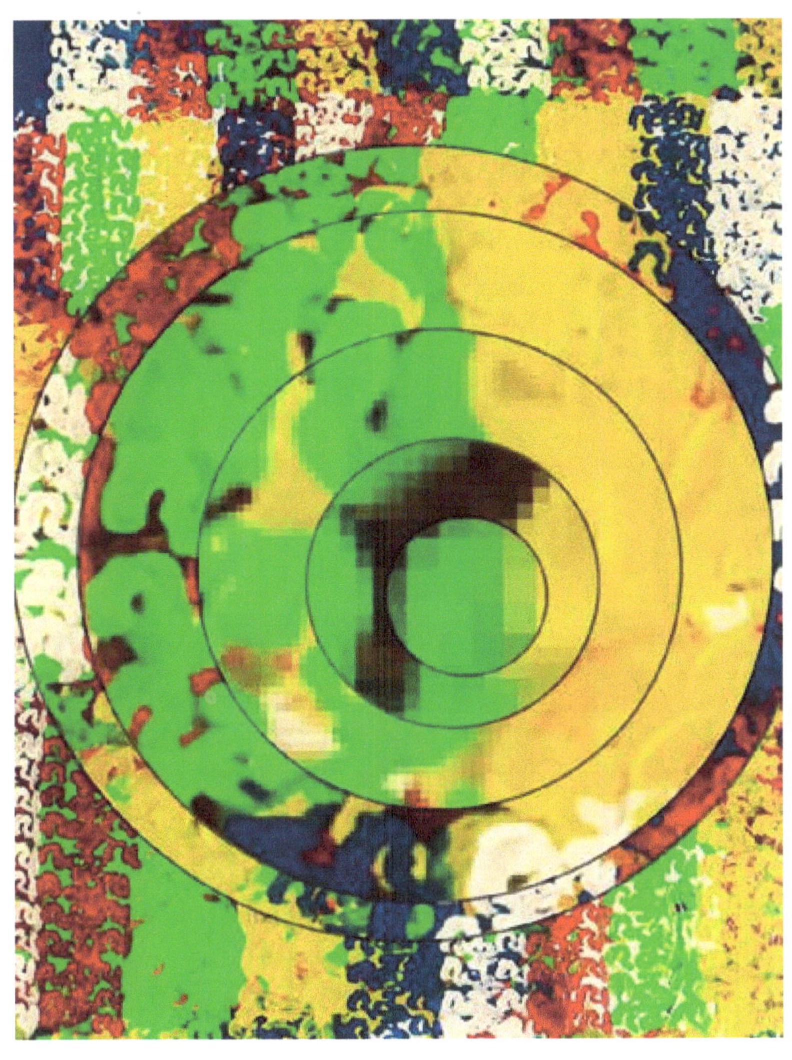

འཚོལ =Searching

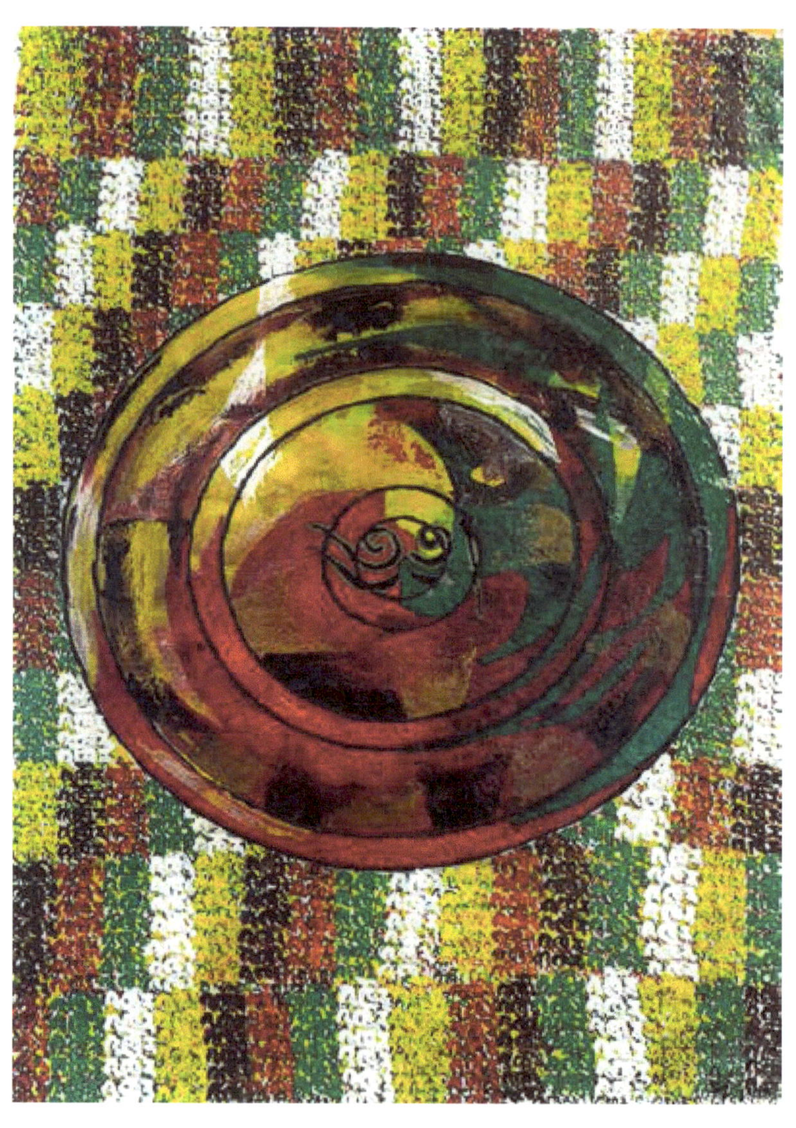

འཁོར་བ། = cycle of life

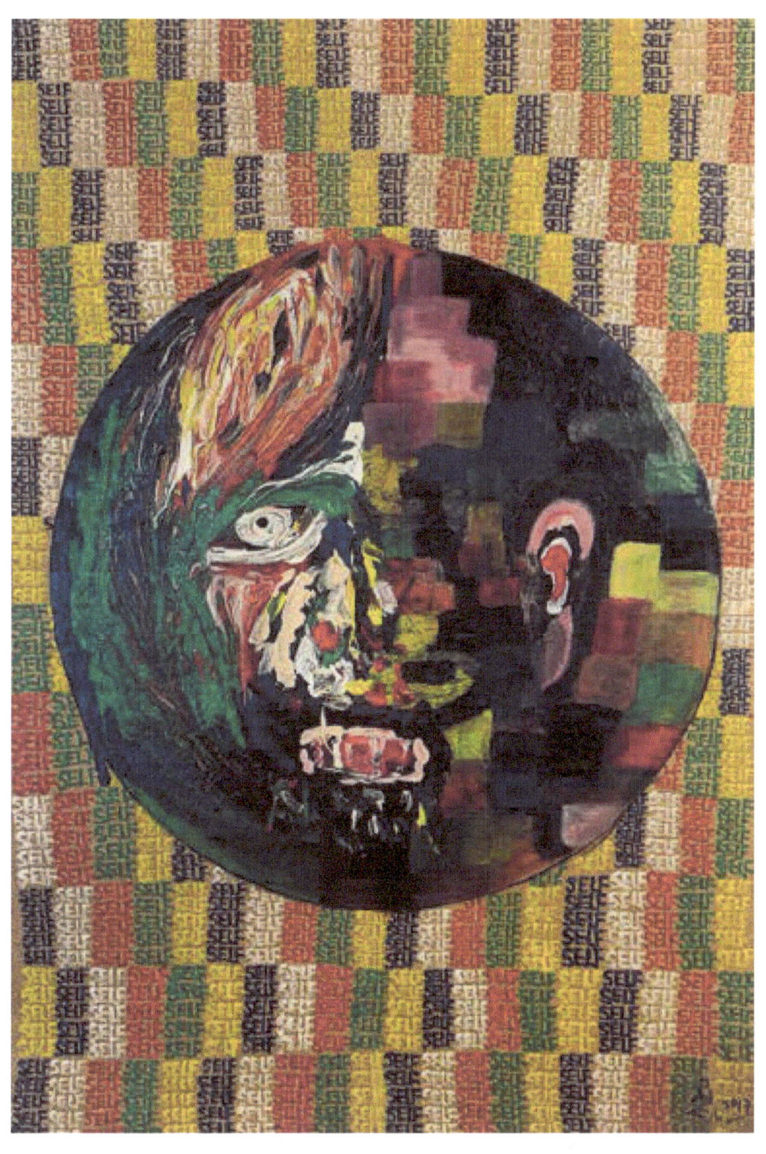

Self/ego

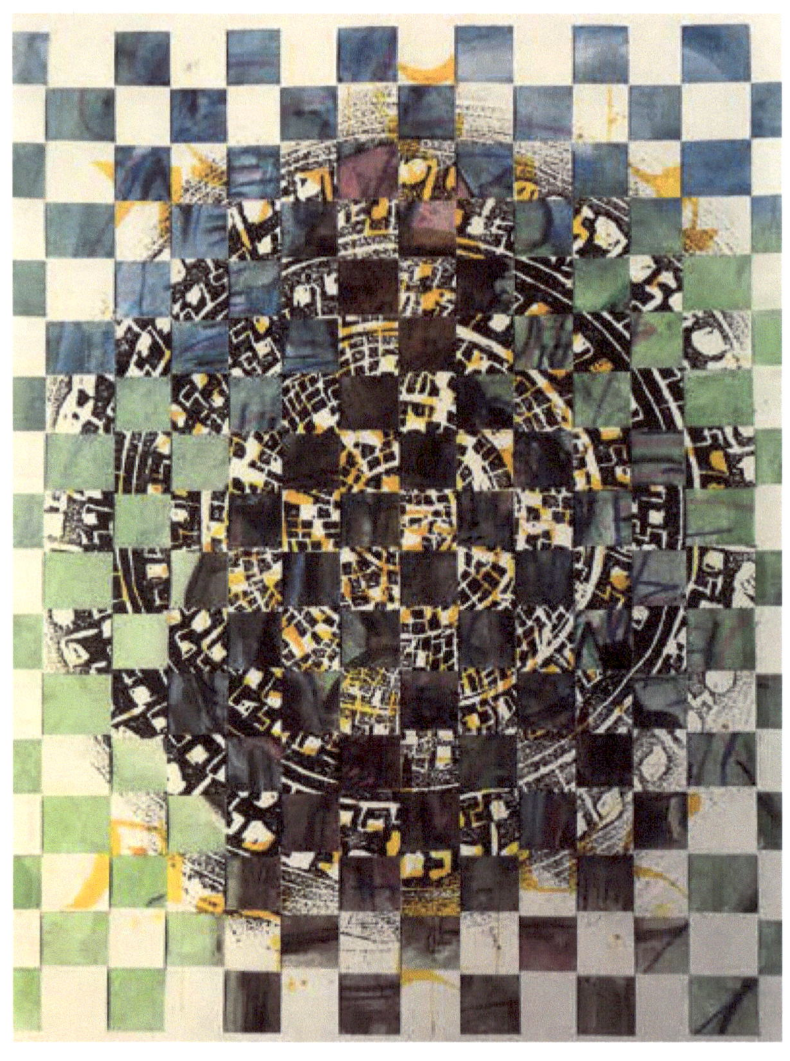

Self-searching

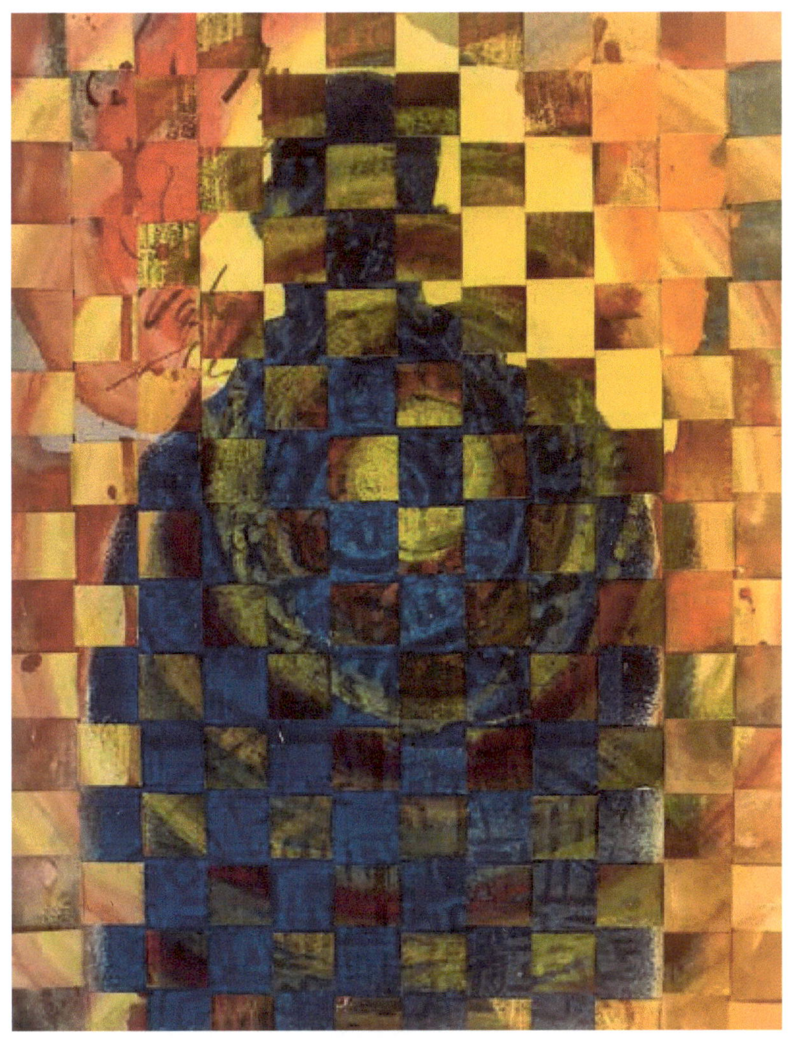

Self-Searching II

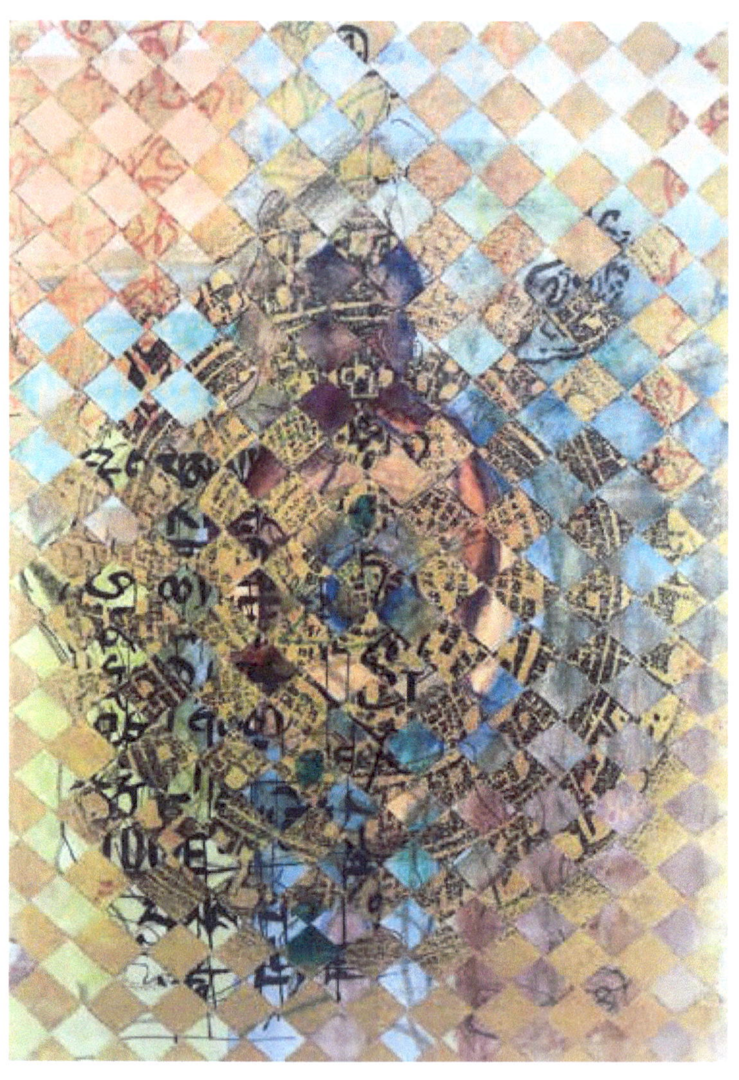

Self-Searching III

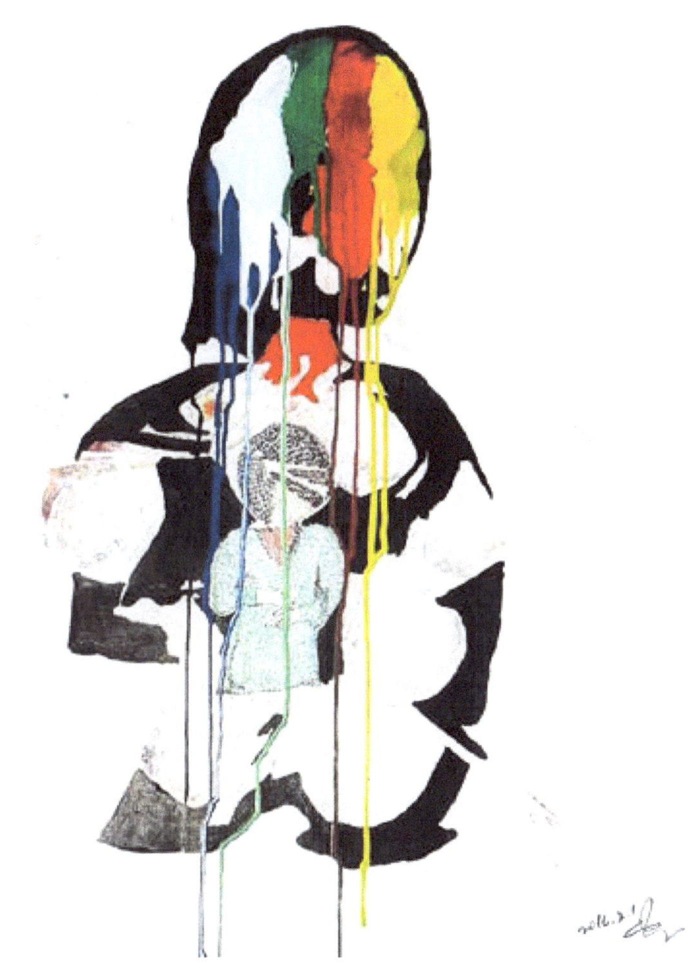

Self within Self

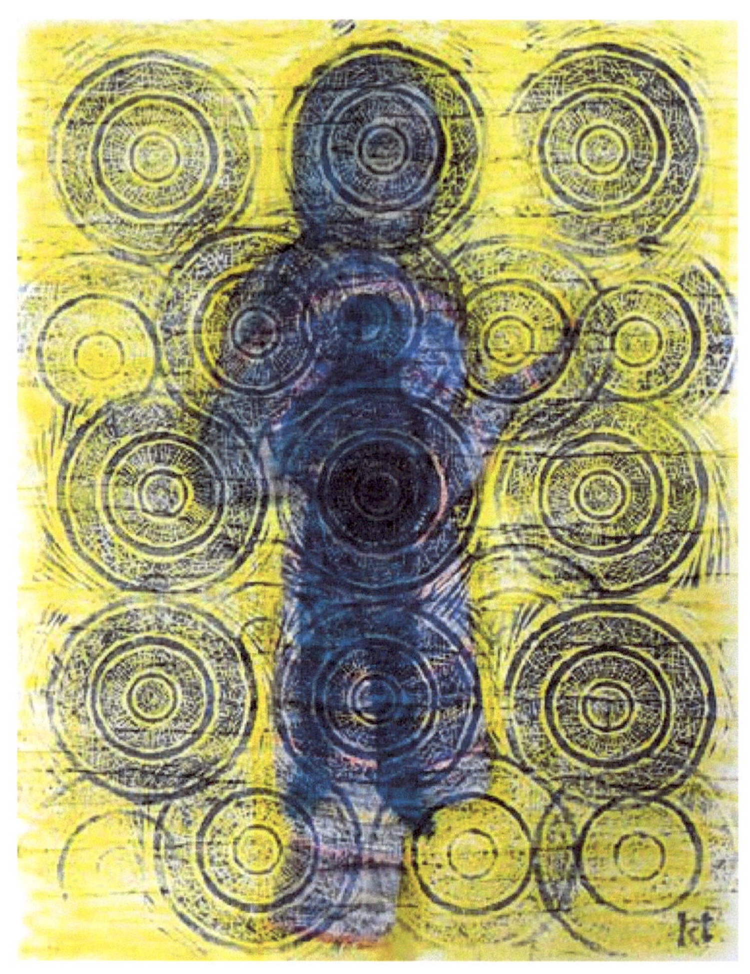

Self within Self II

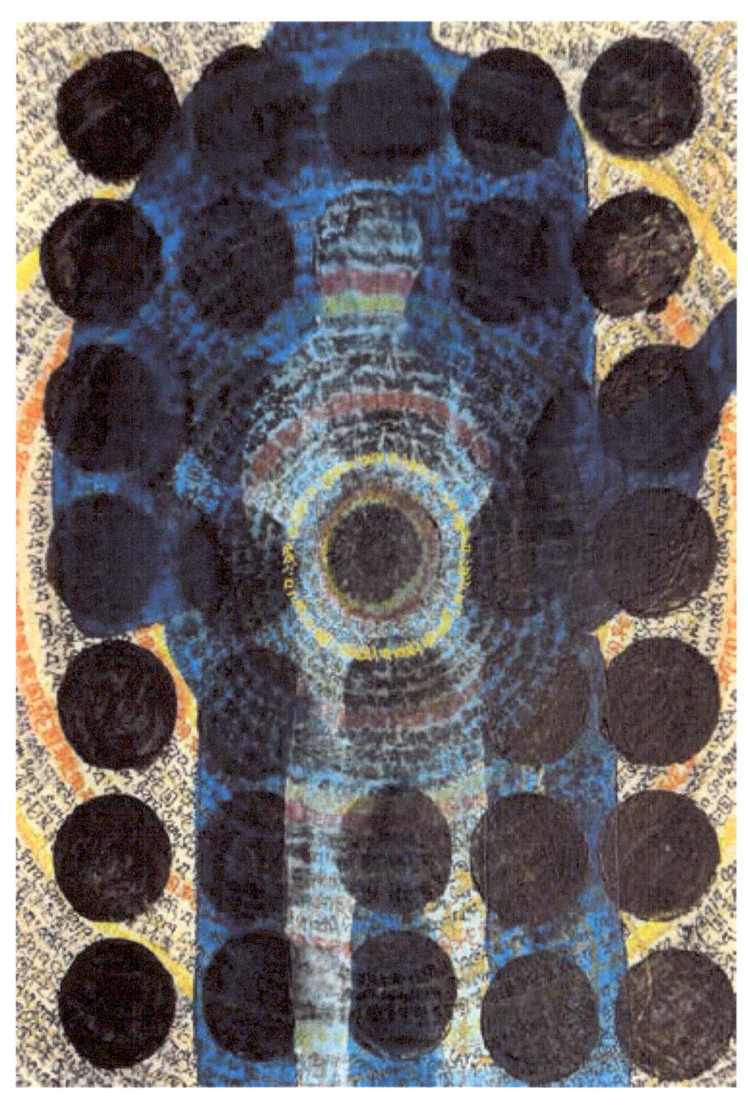

Self within Self III

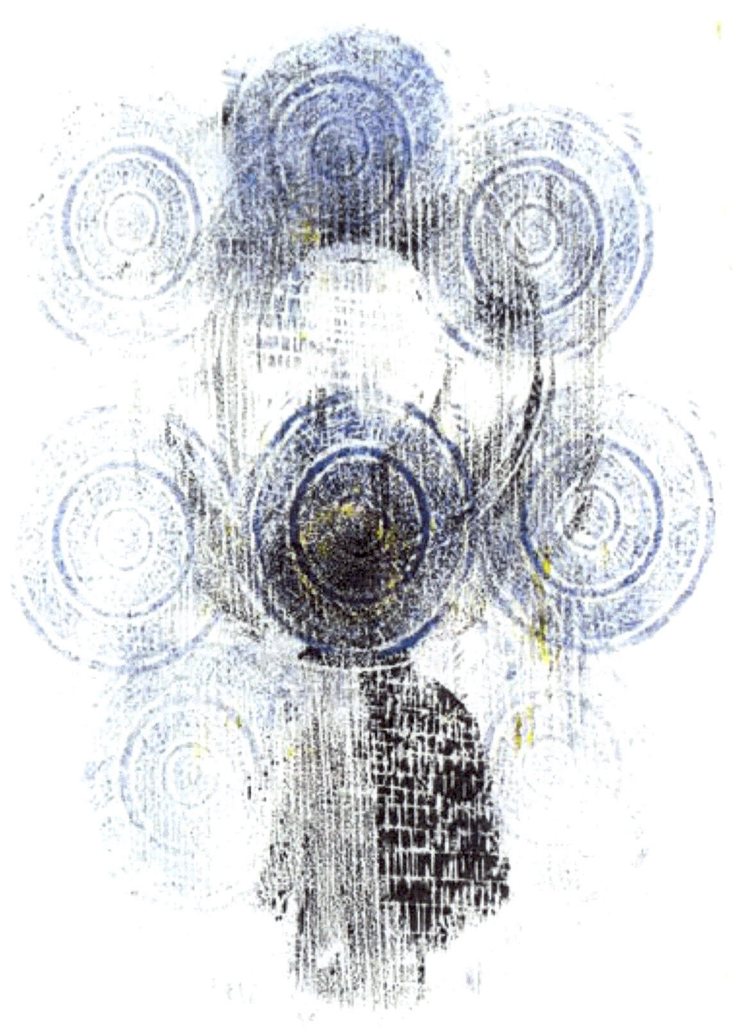

Untitled

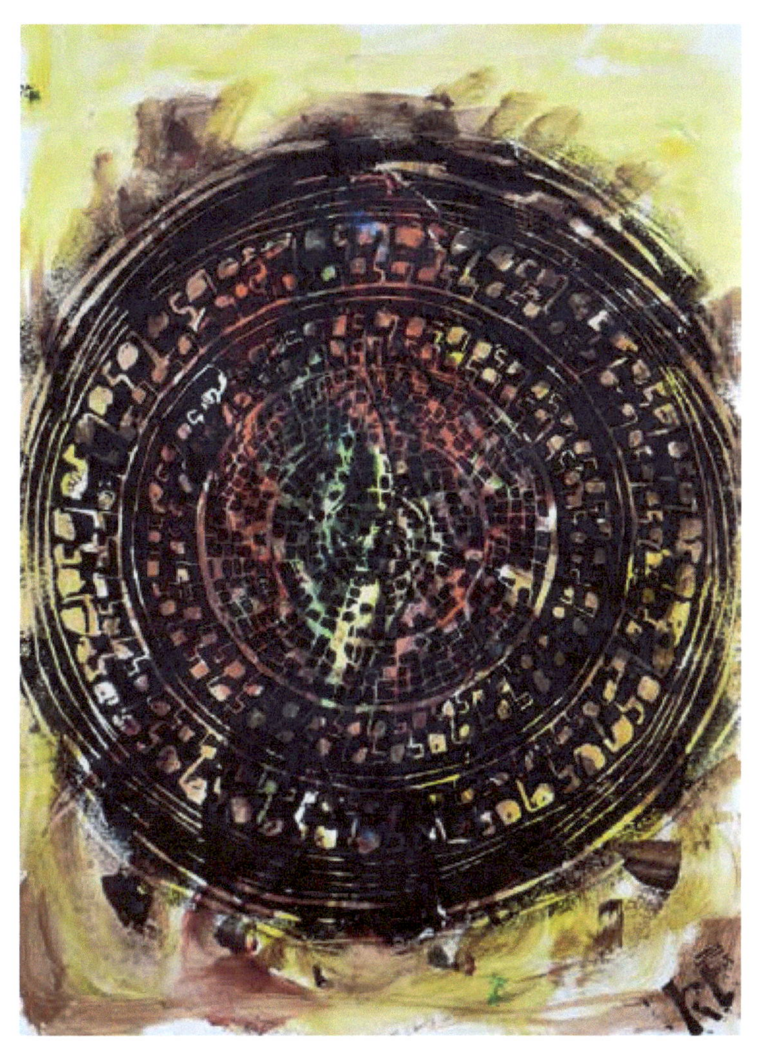

Self -awareness

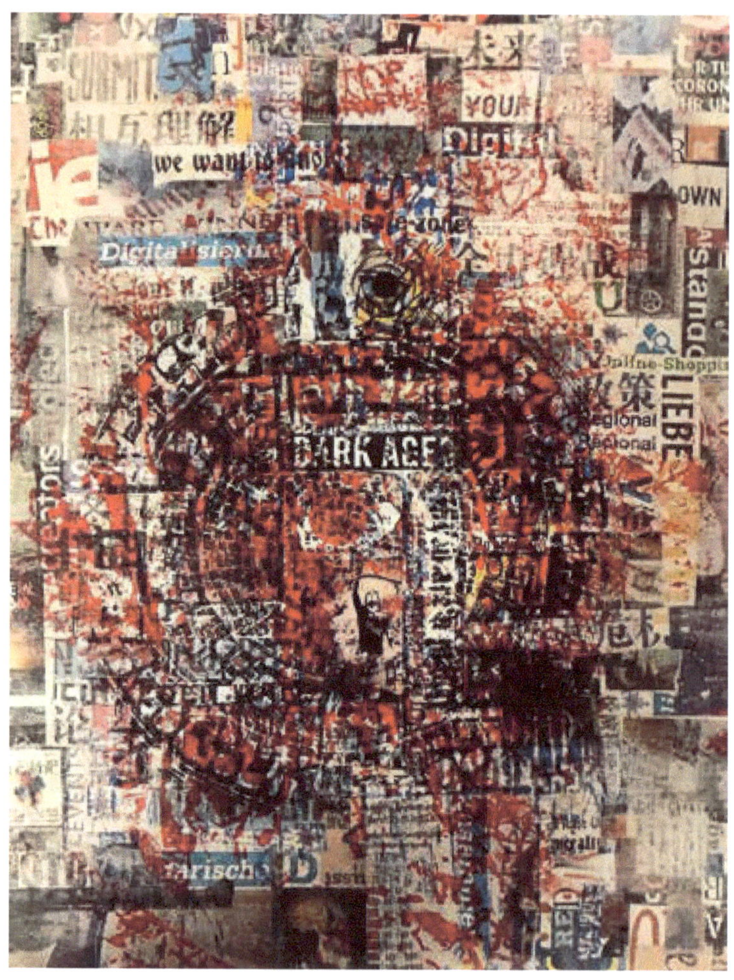

Dark age

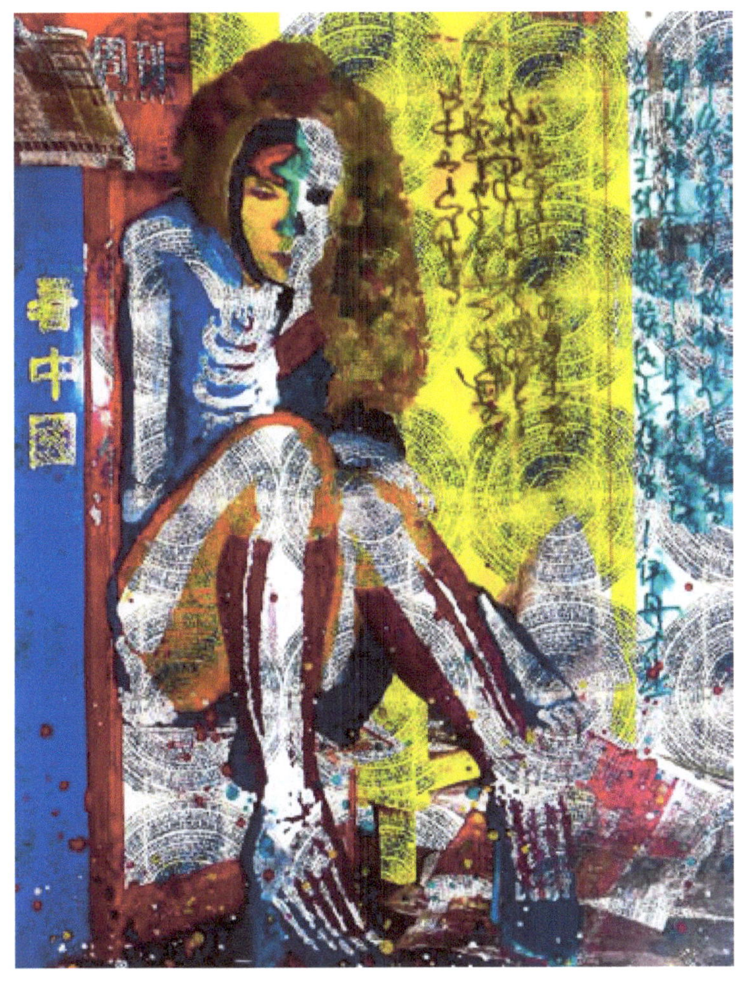

Watching

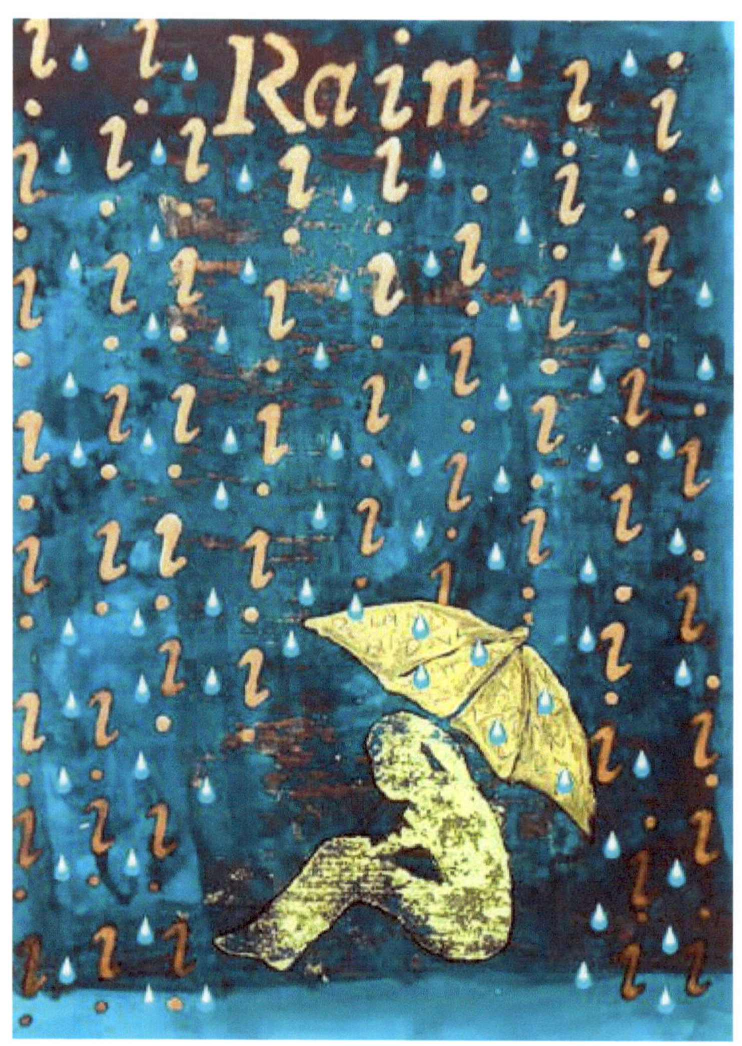

Rain

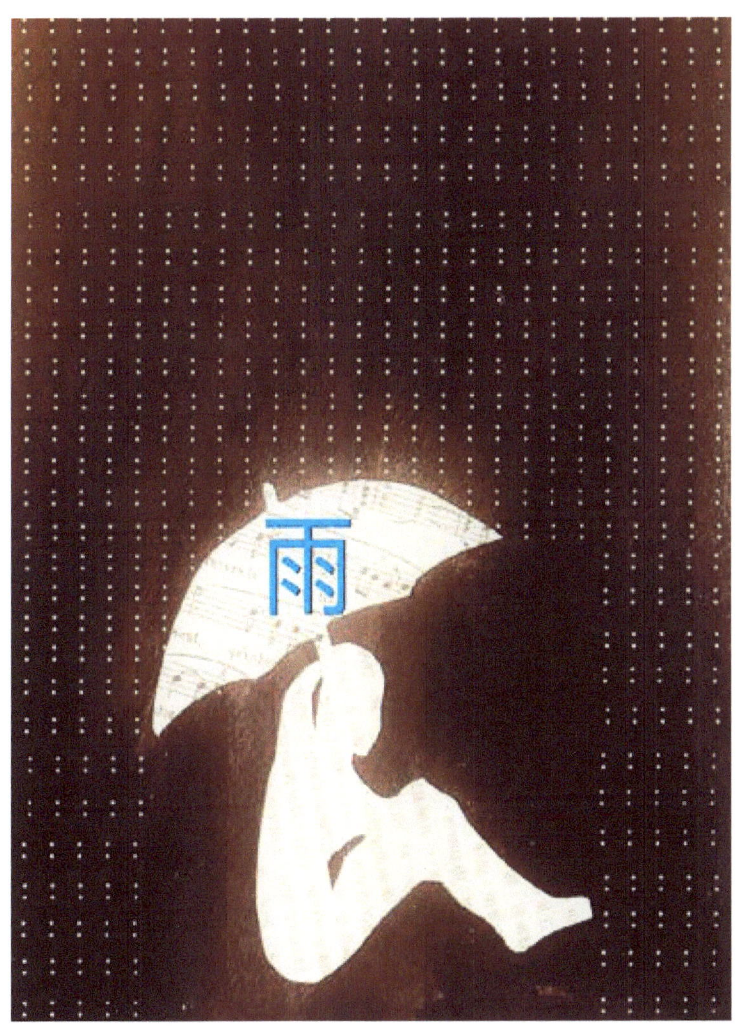

雨 = Rain

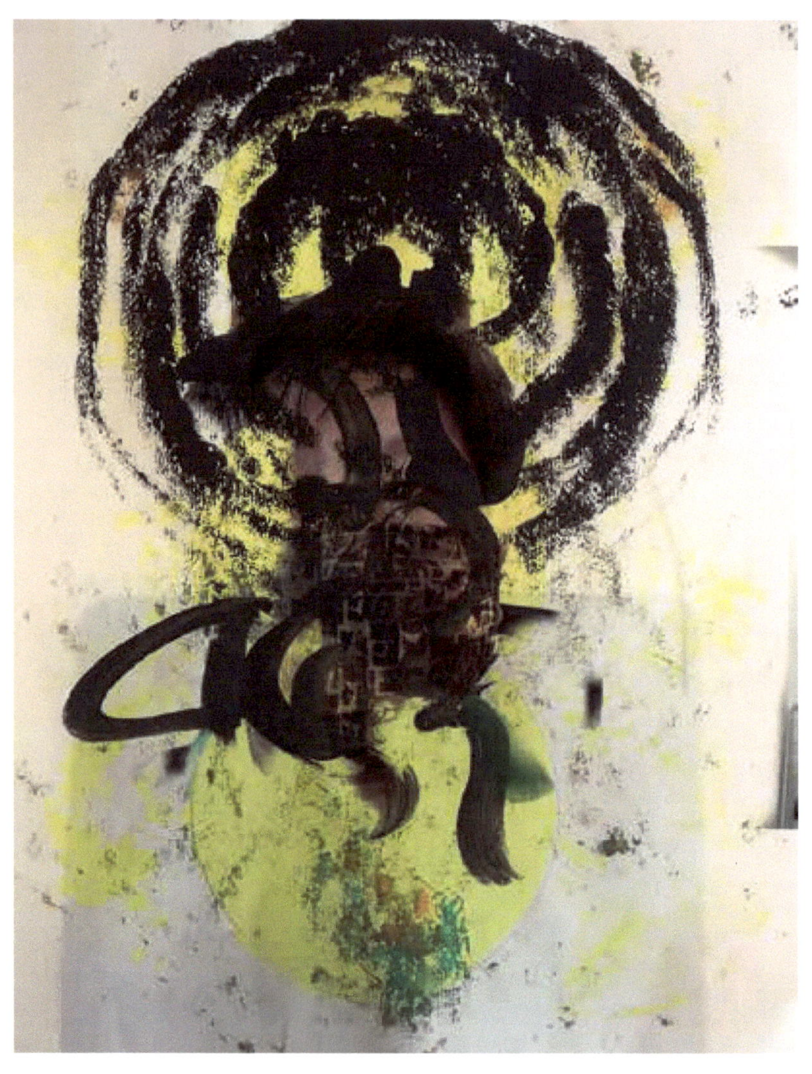

Year of Mask

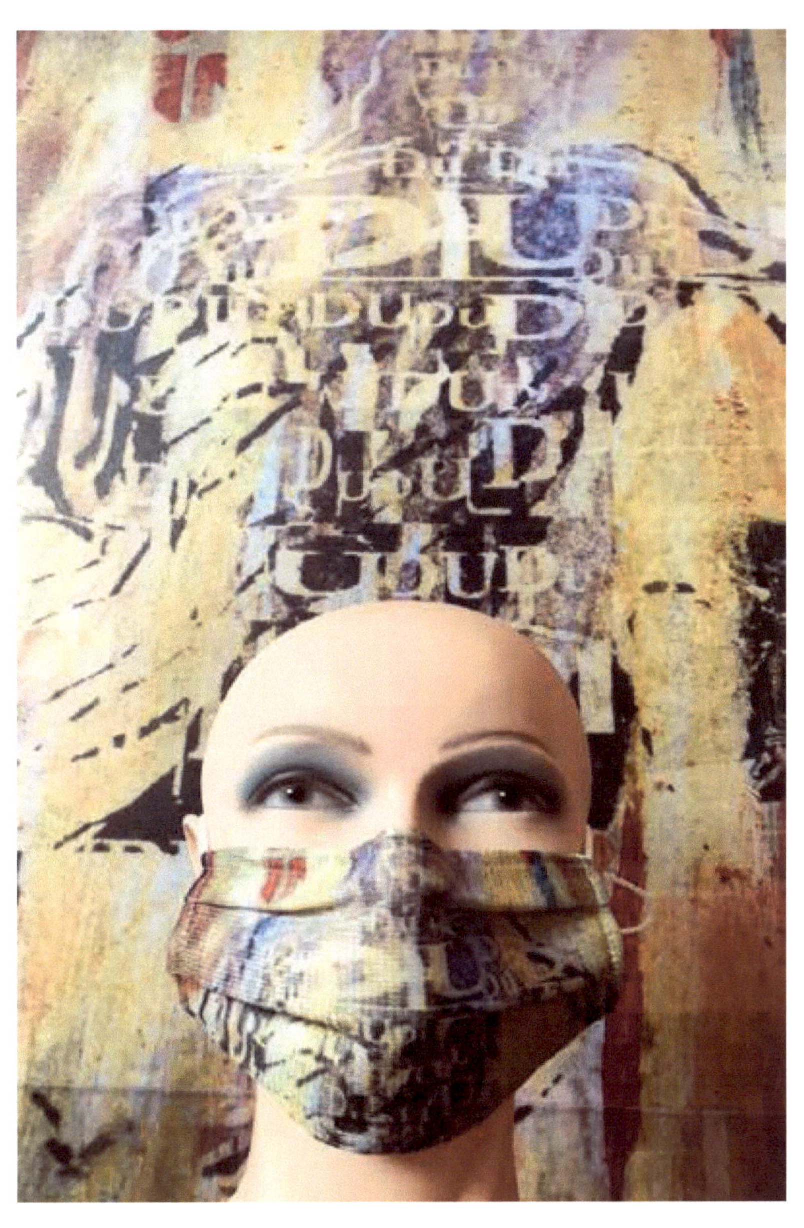

Year of Mask II

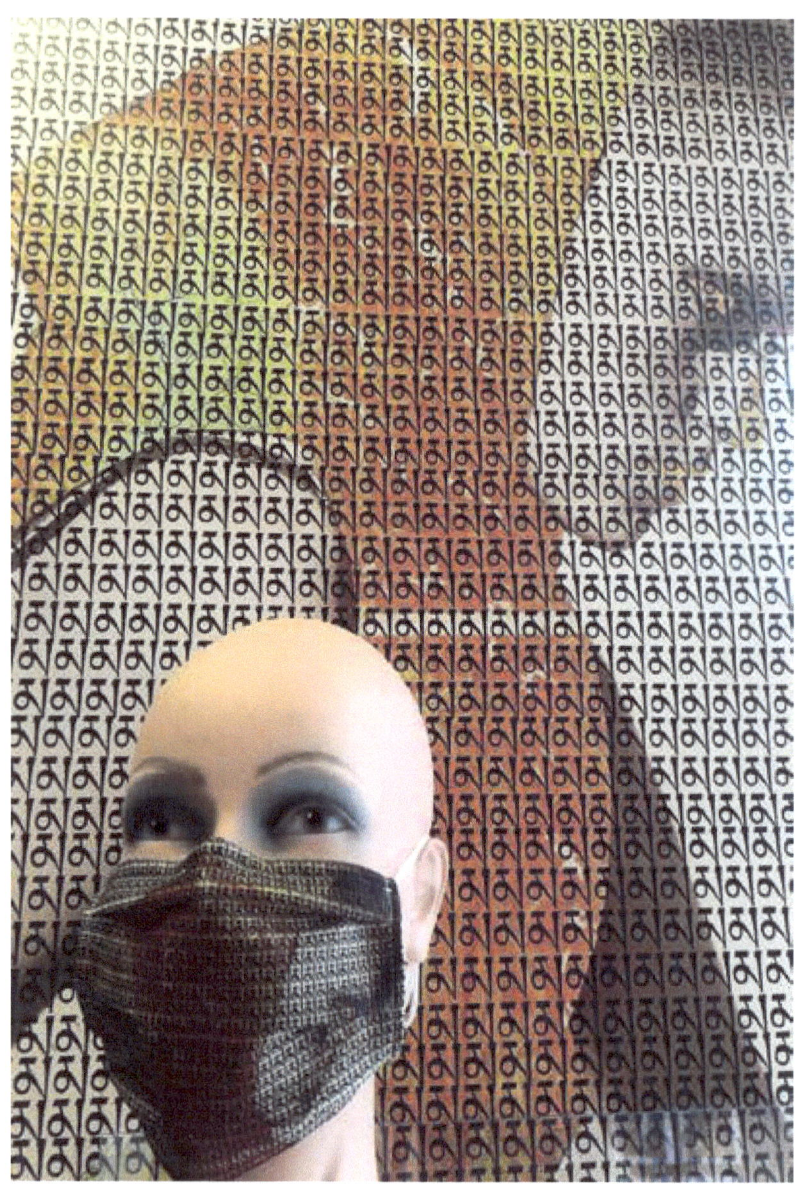

Year of Mask III

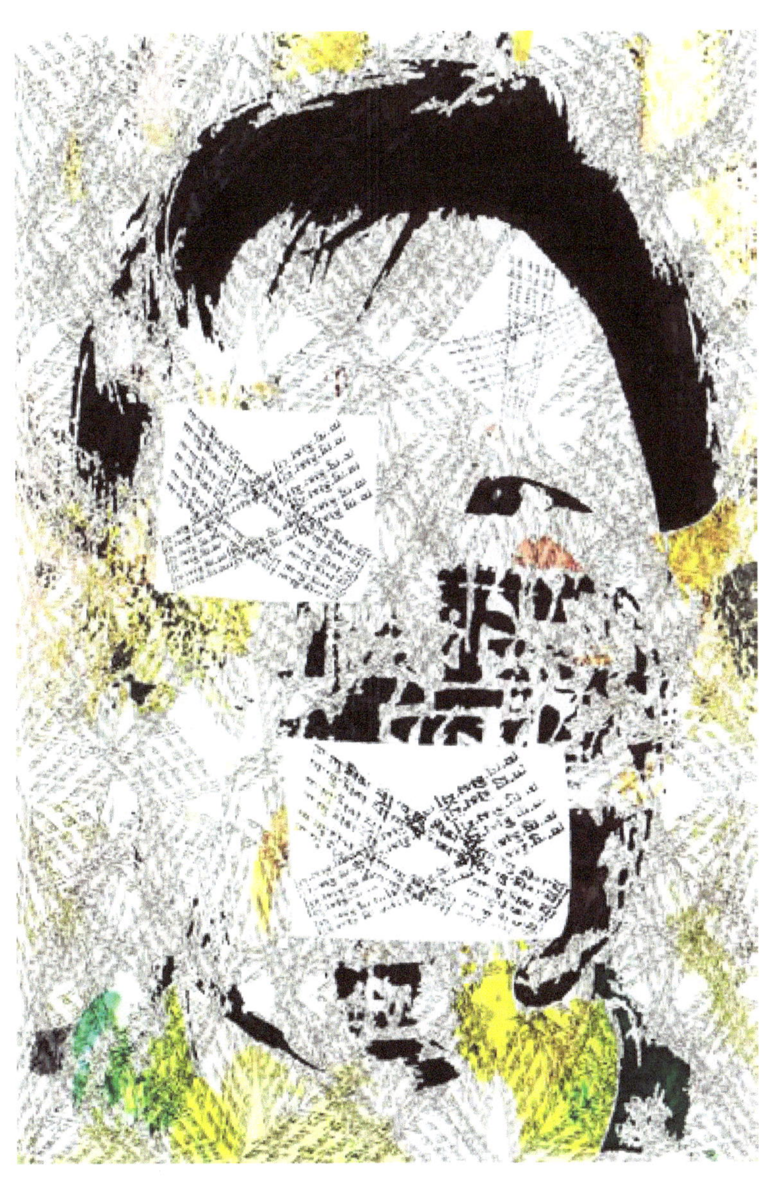

Year of Mask IV

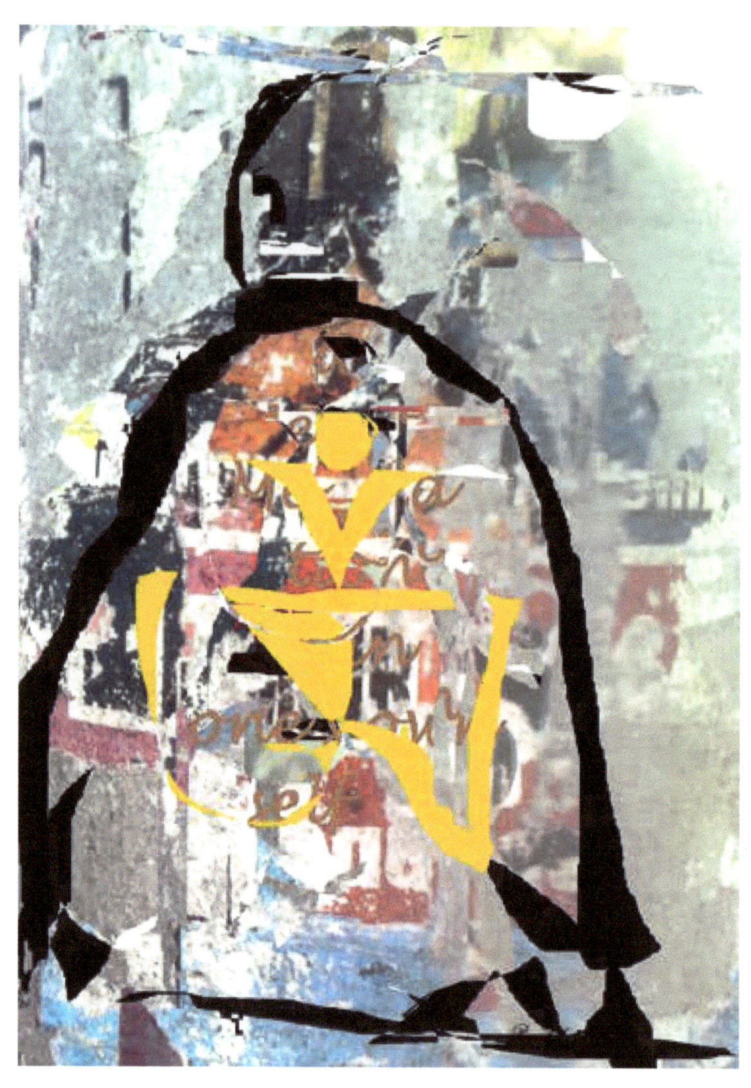

Meditation

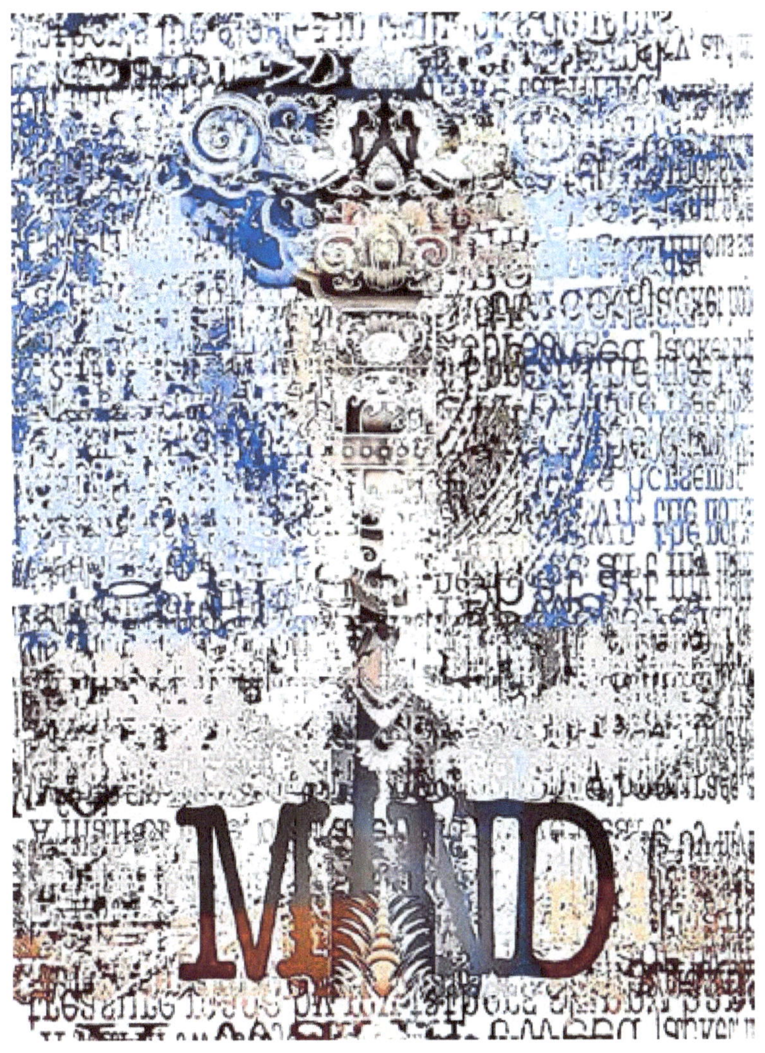

mind

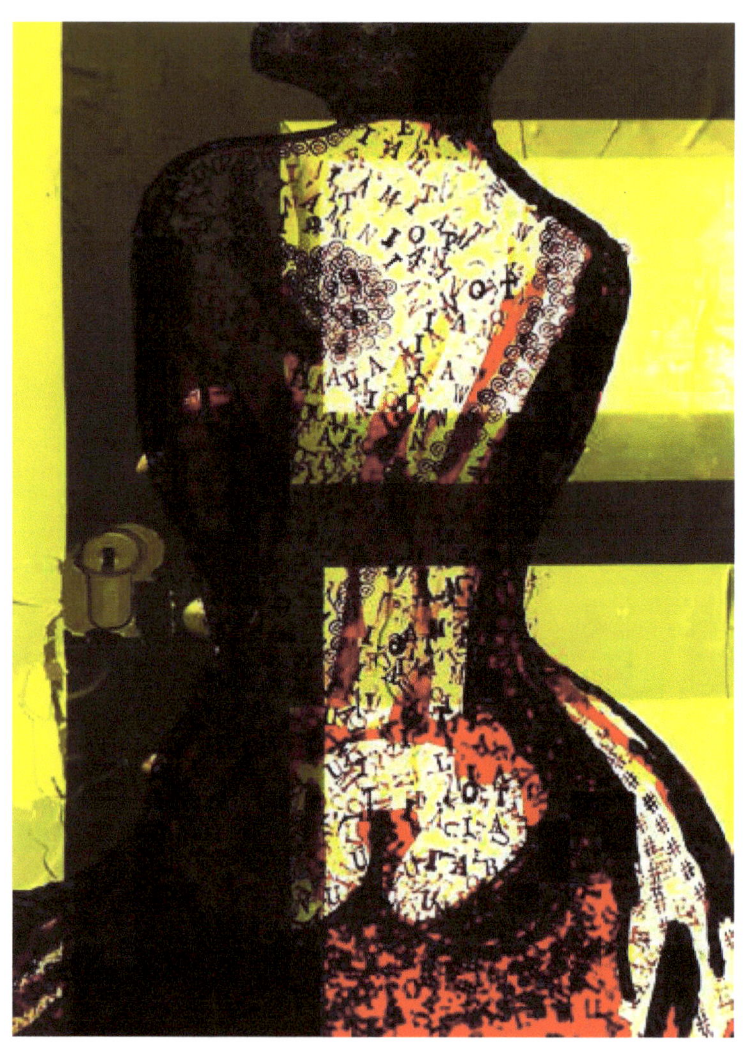

Self -clock within

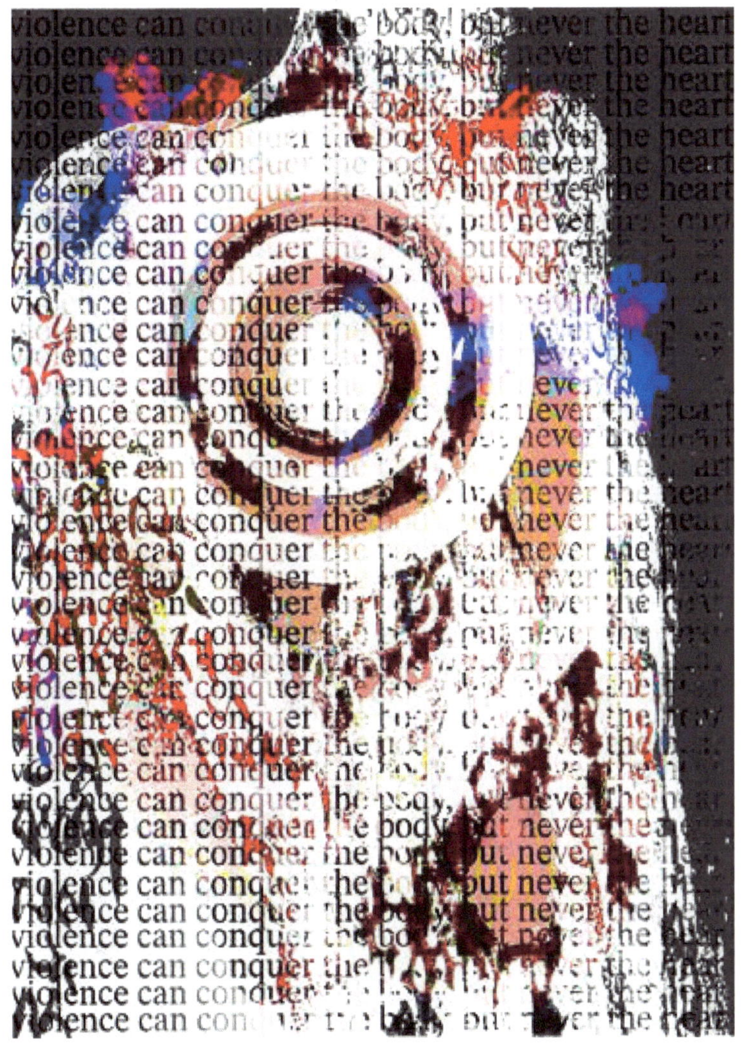

Violence can conquer the body
But never heart

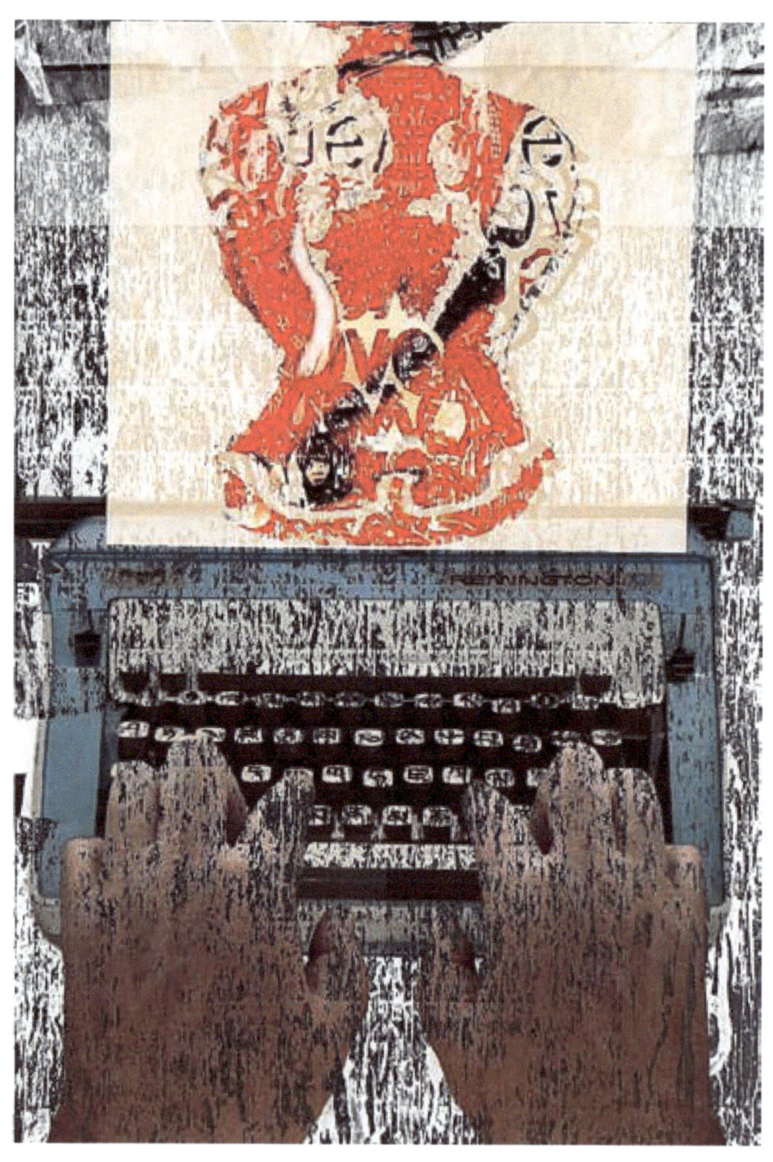

Over (old Tibetan typing writer)

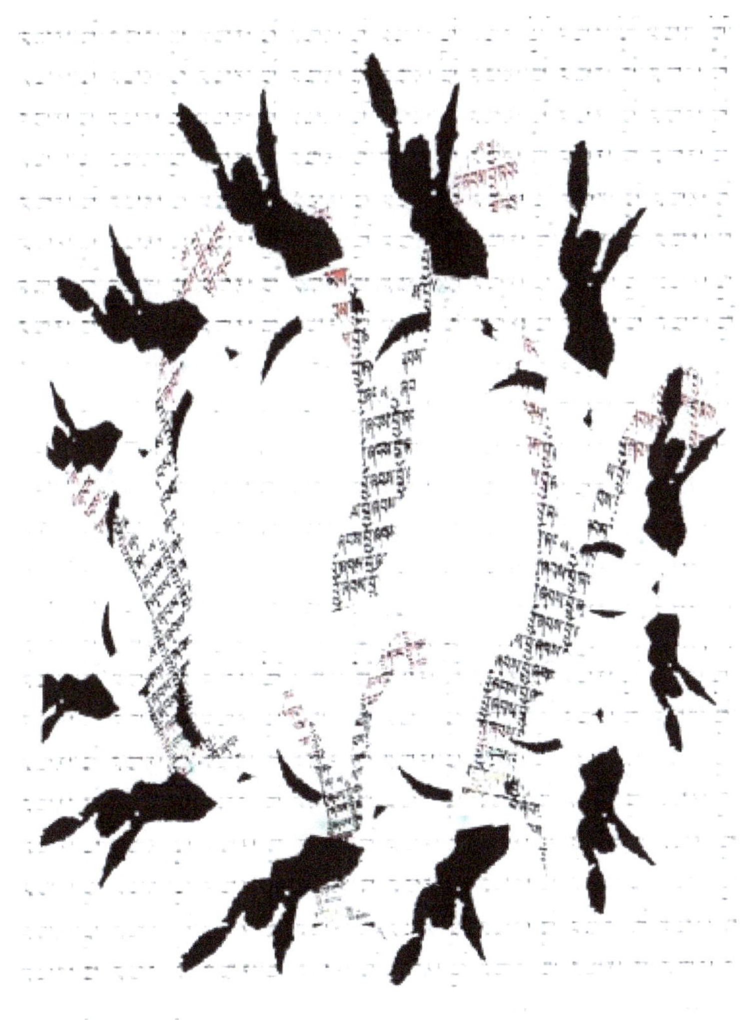

Dance

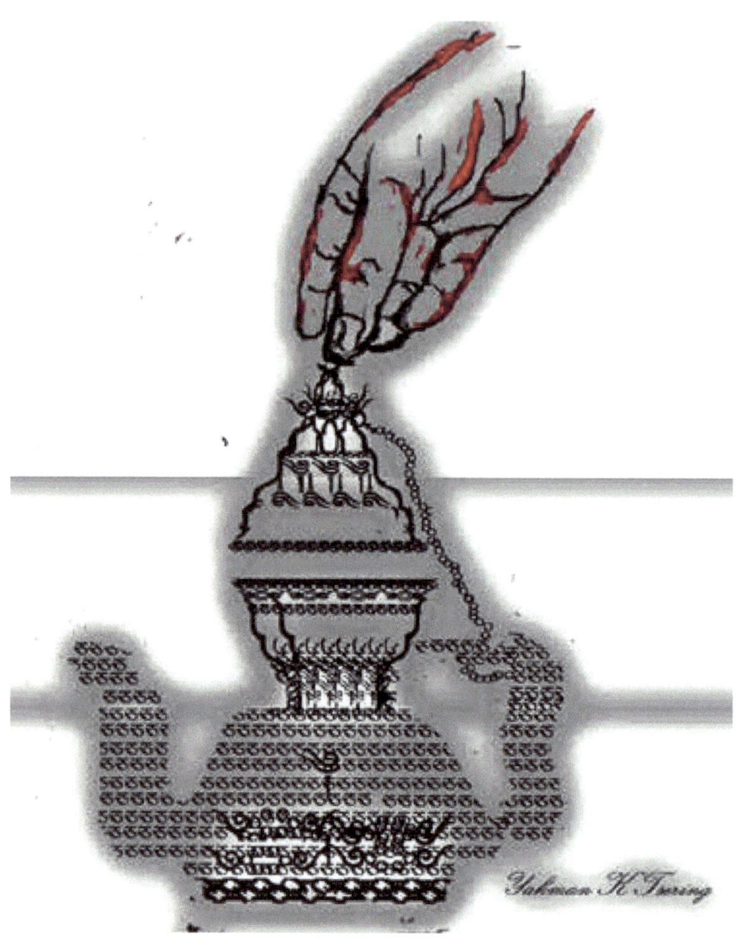

Tibetan Teapot

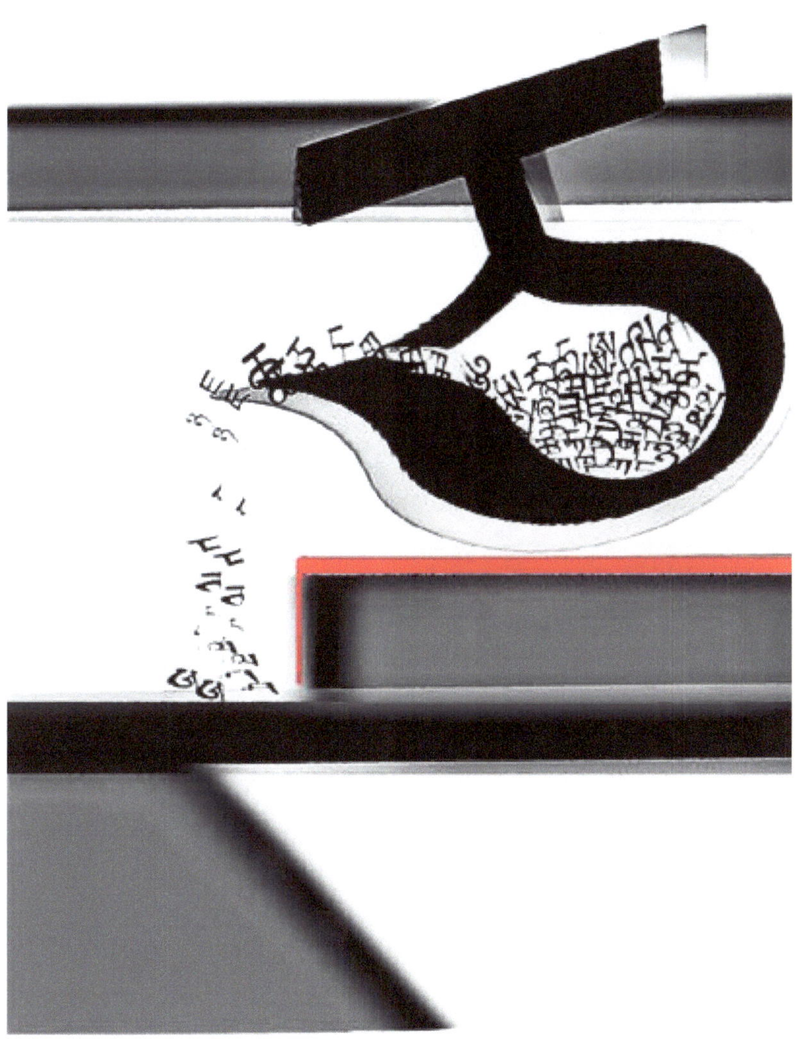

Tibetan Tea

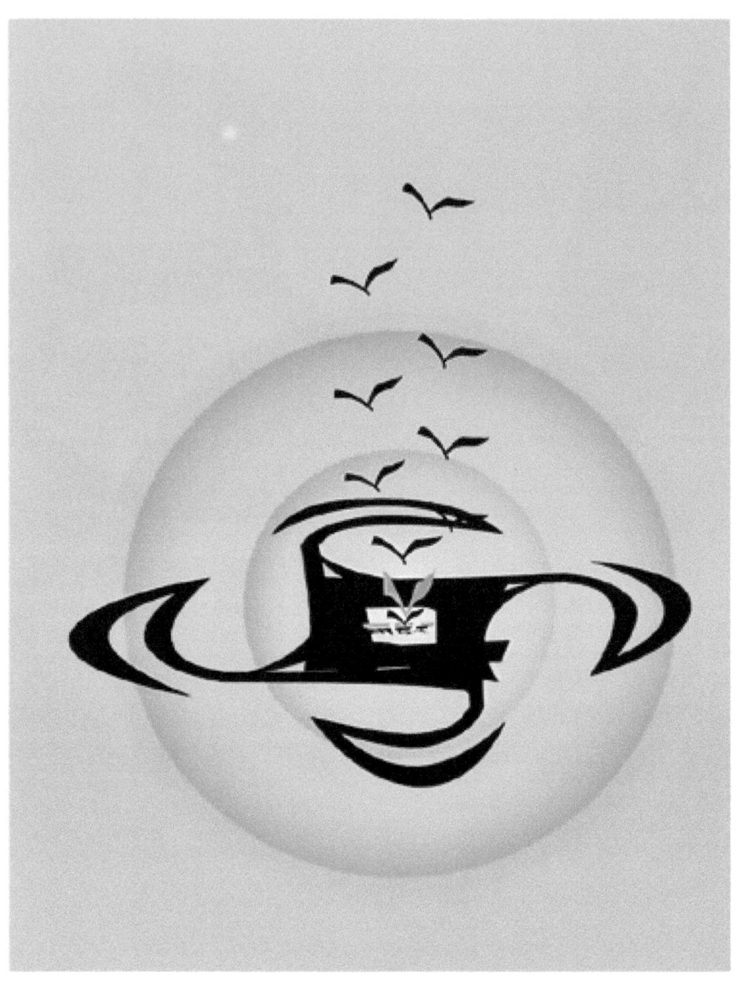

Sky burial

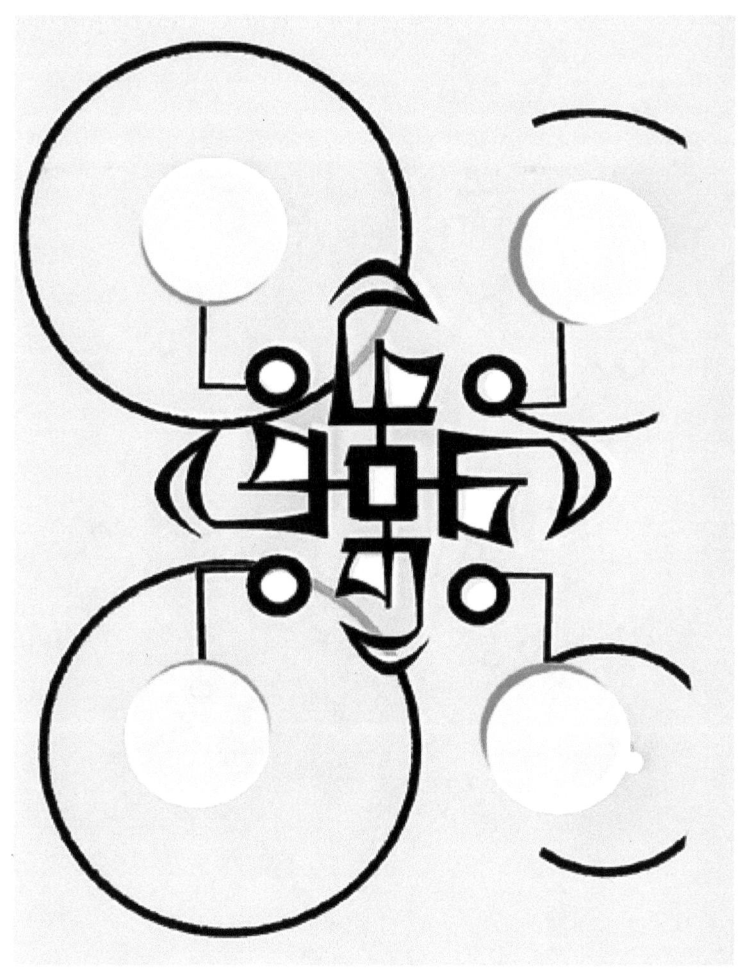

Back

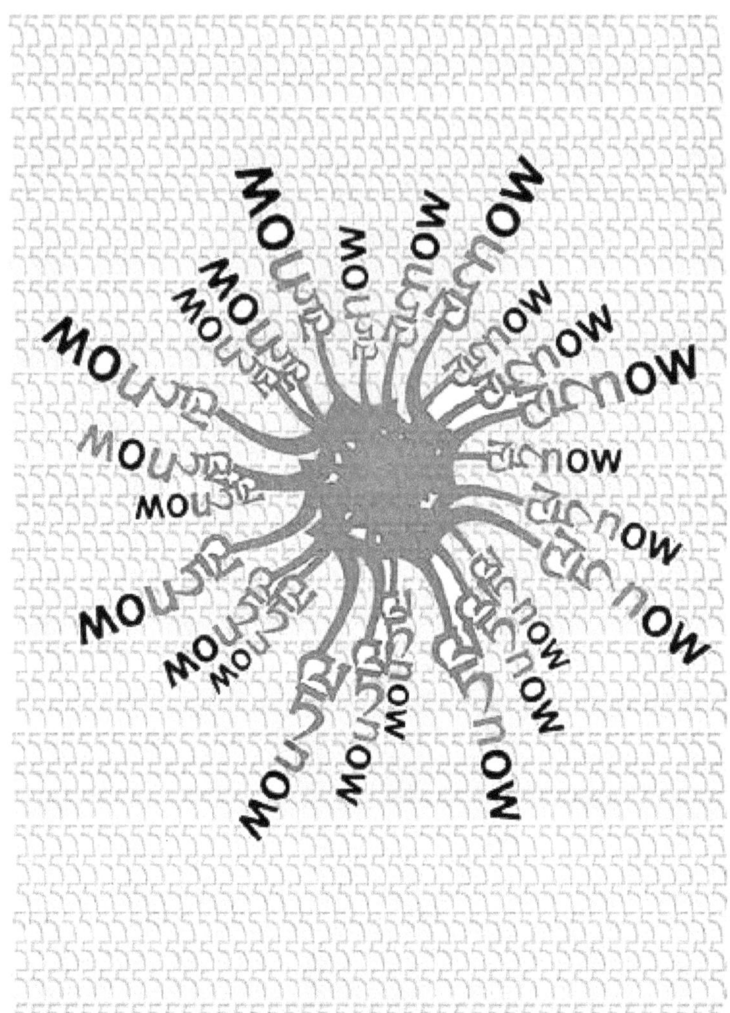

Now

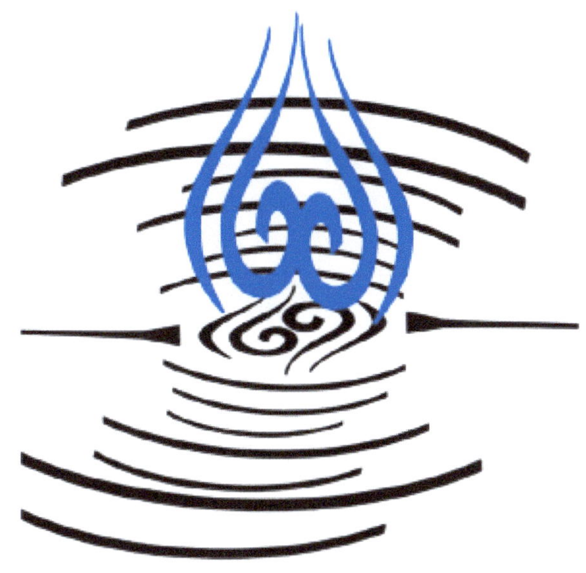

Waterdrop

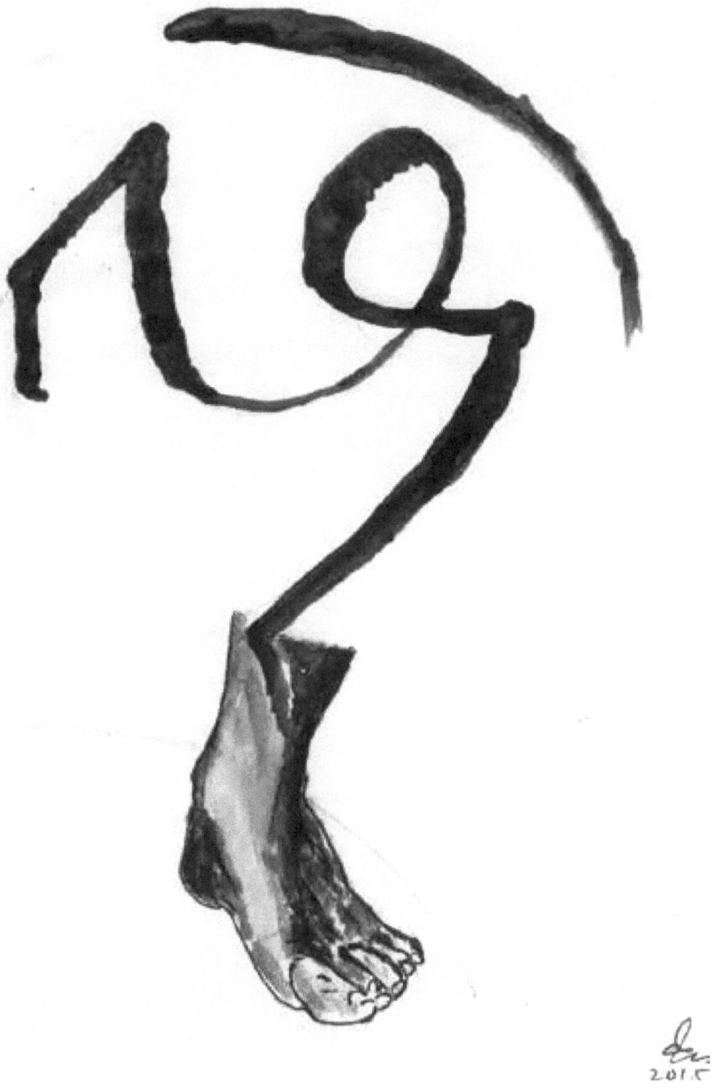

Walking

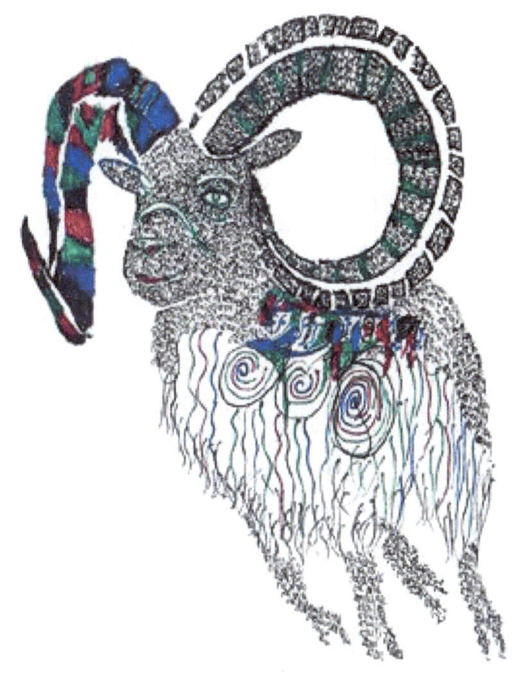

Year of Goat

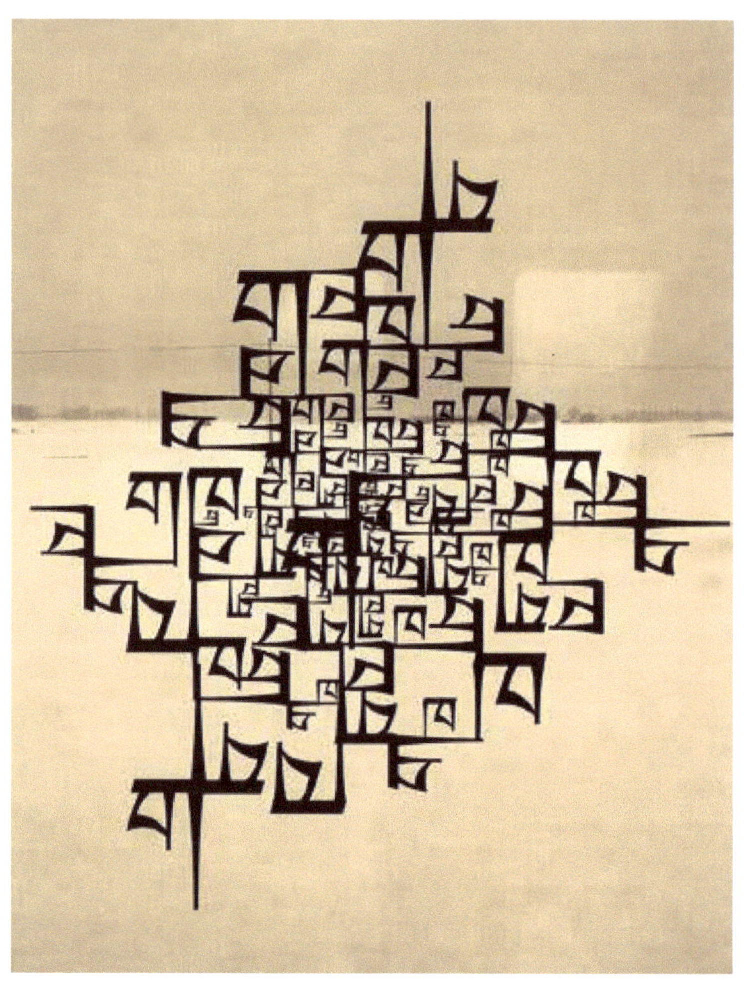

Untitled

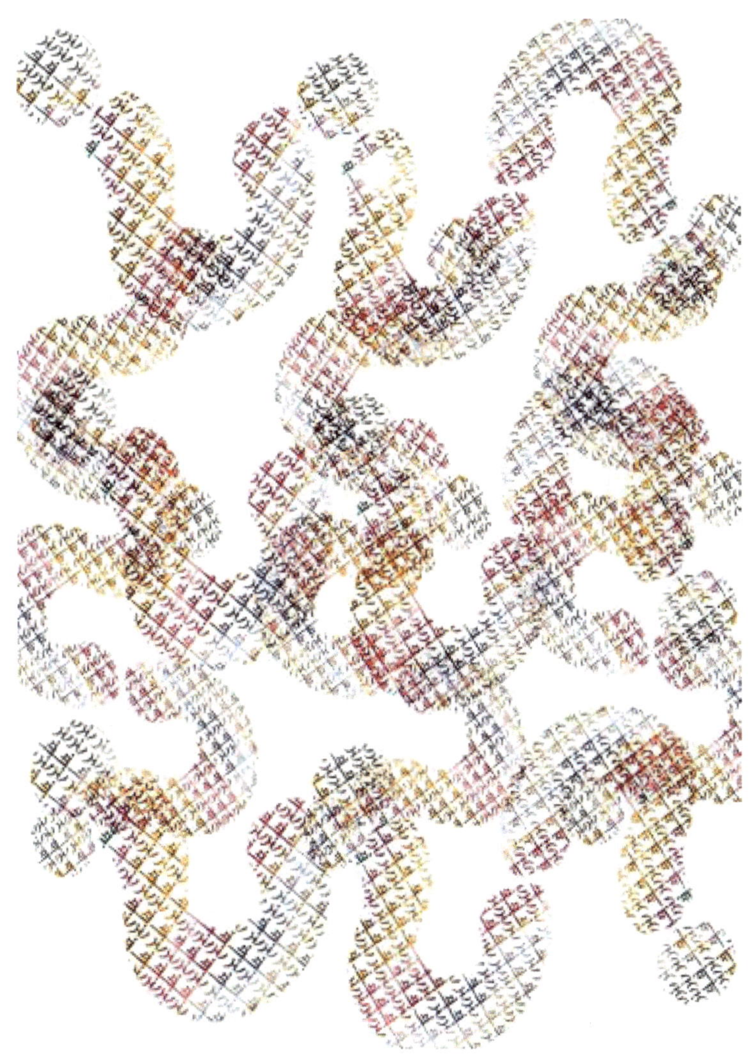

Question

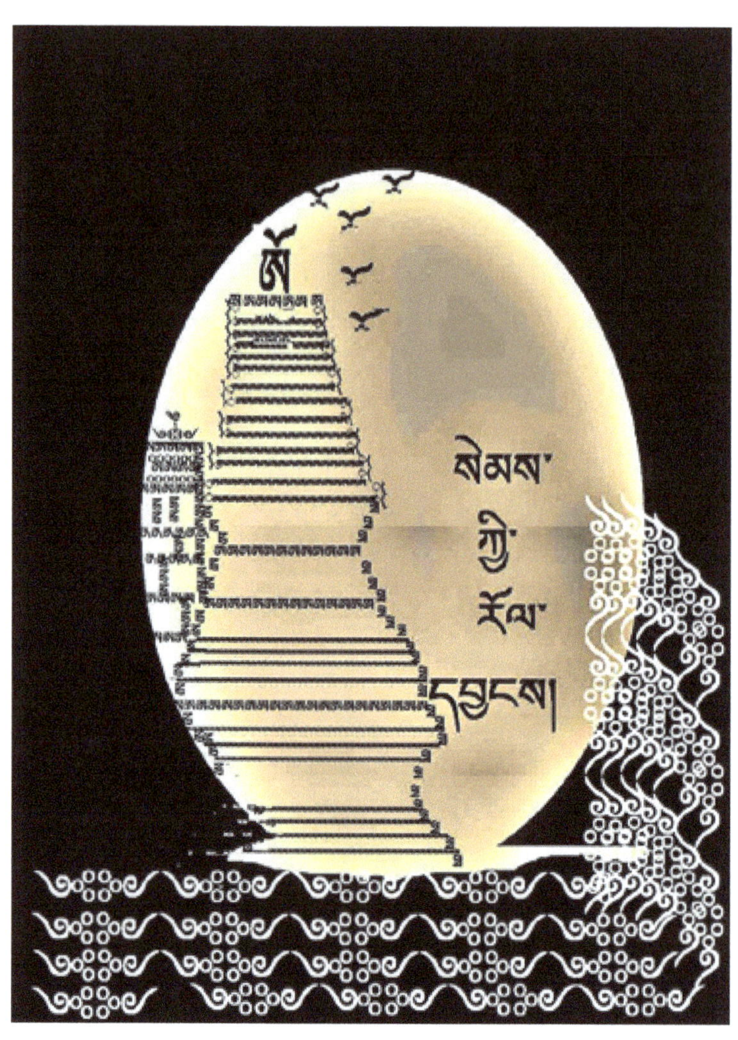

Rhythm of heart

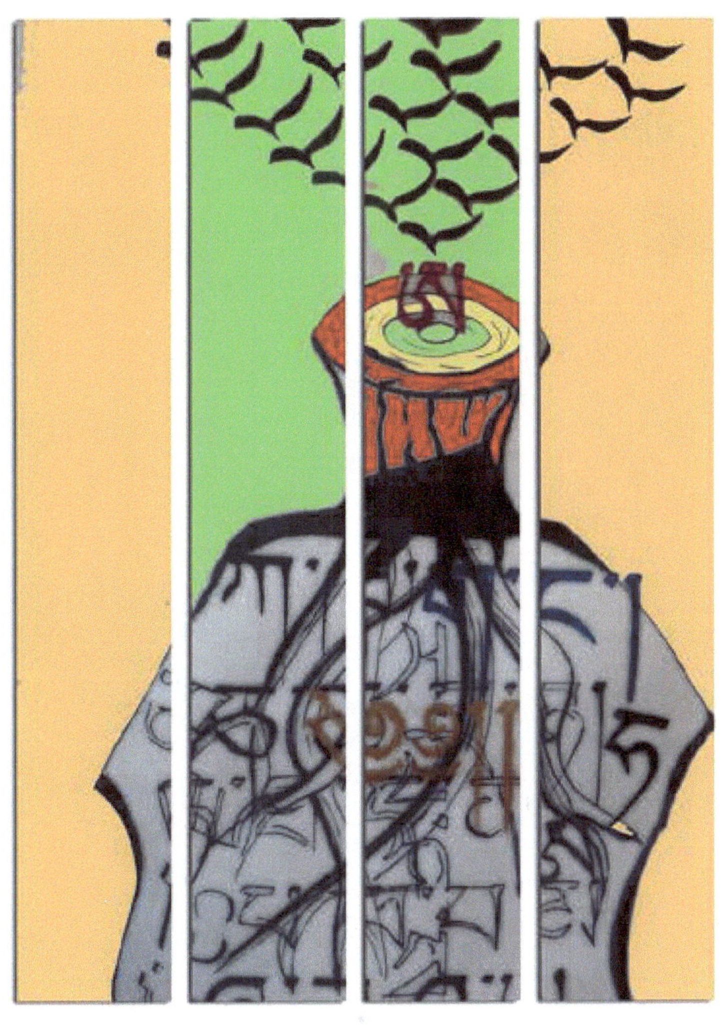

Untitled

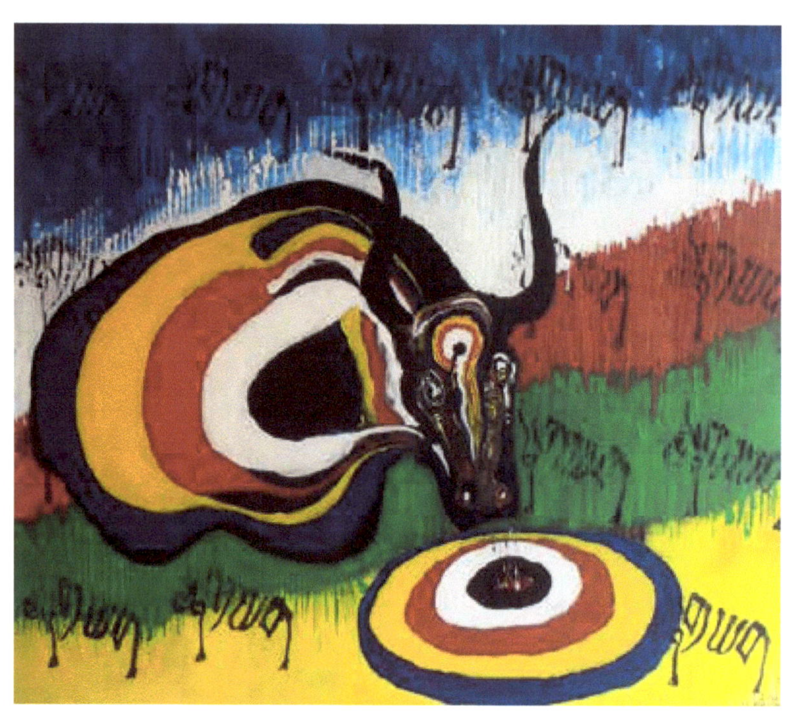

Yak Elegy

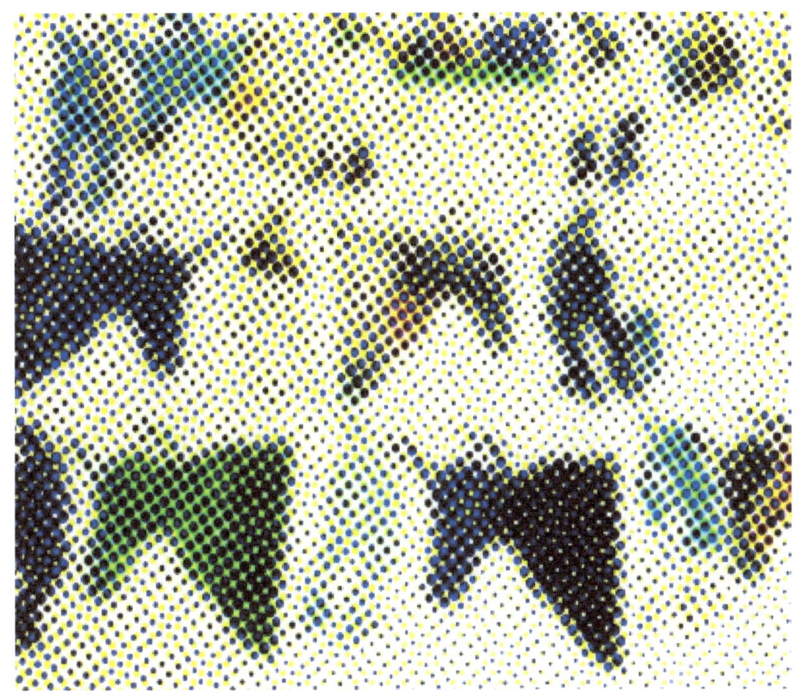

Yak Playing

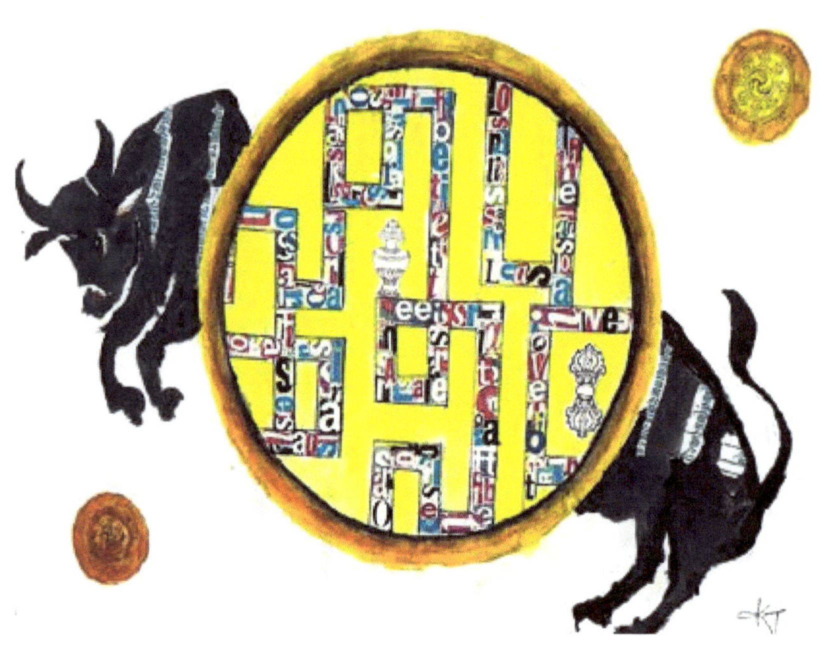

Iron Bull Year

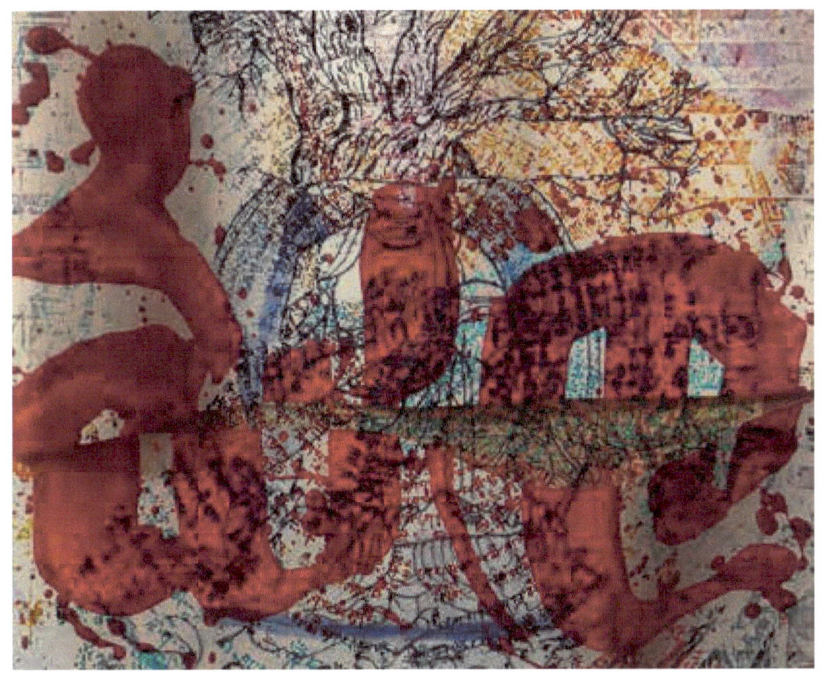

Wound

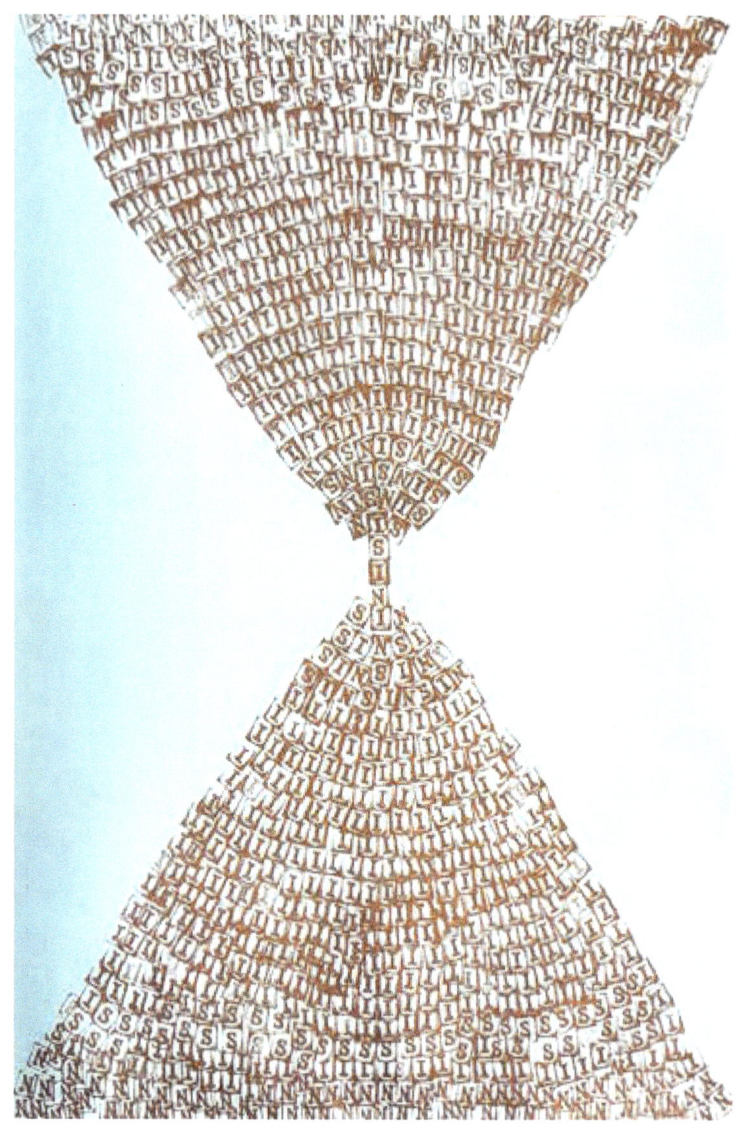

Sin

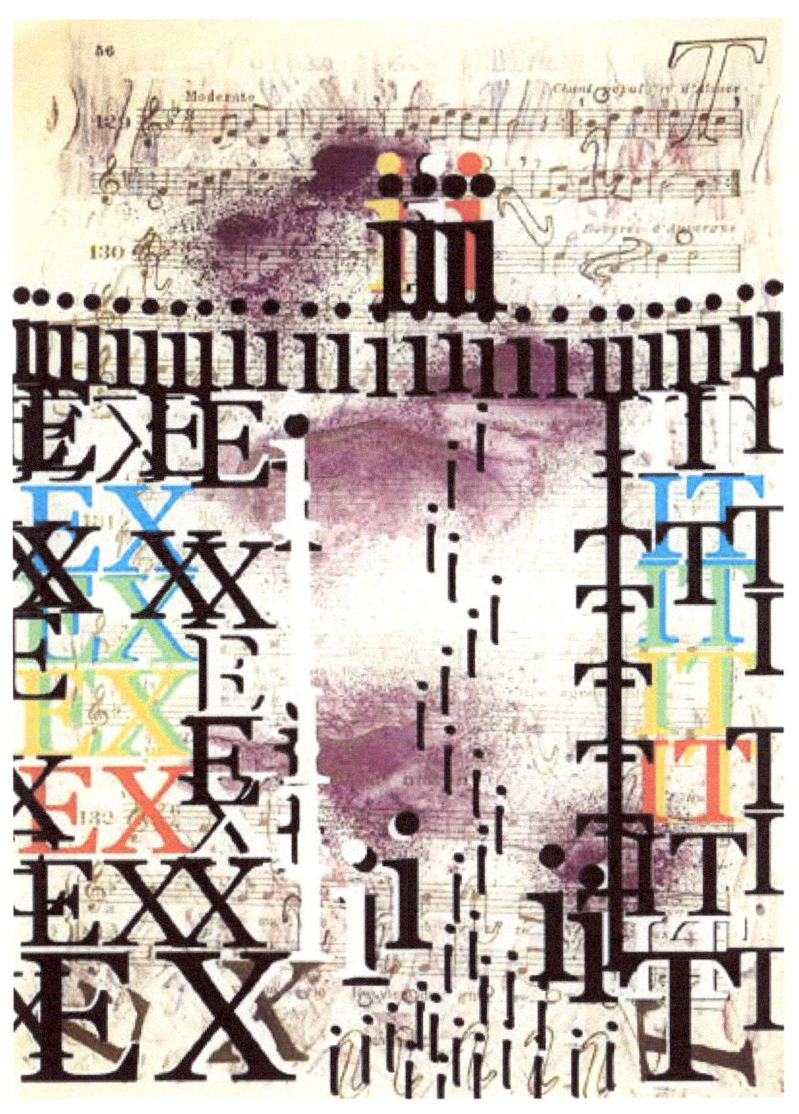

Exit

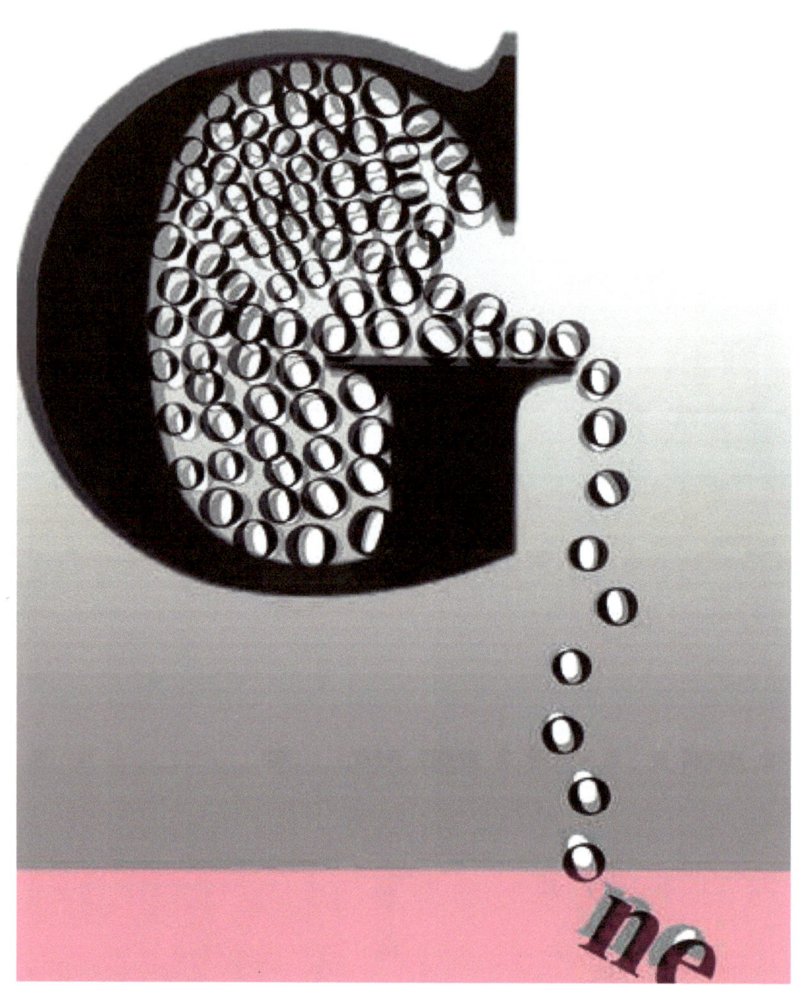

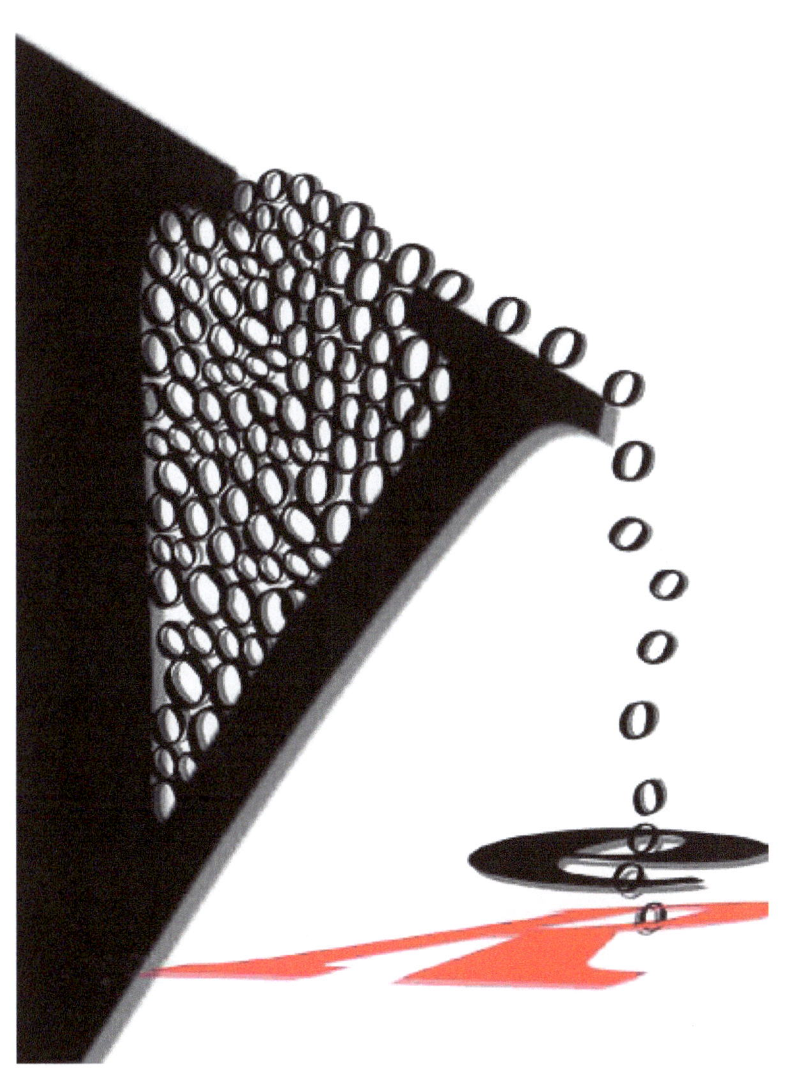

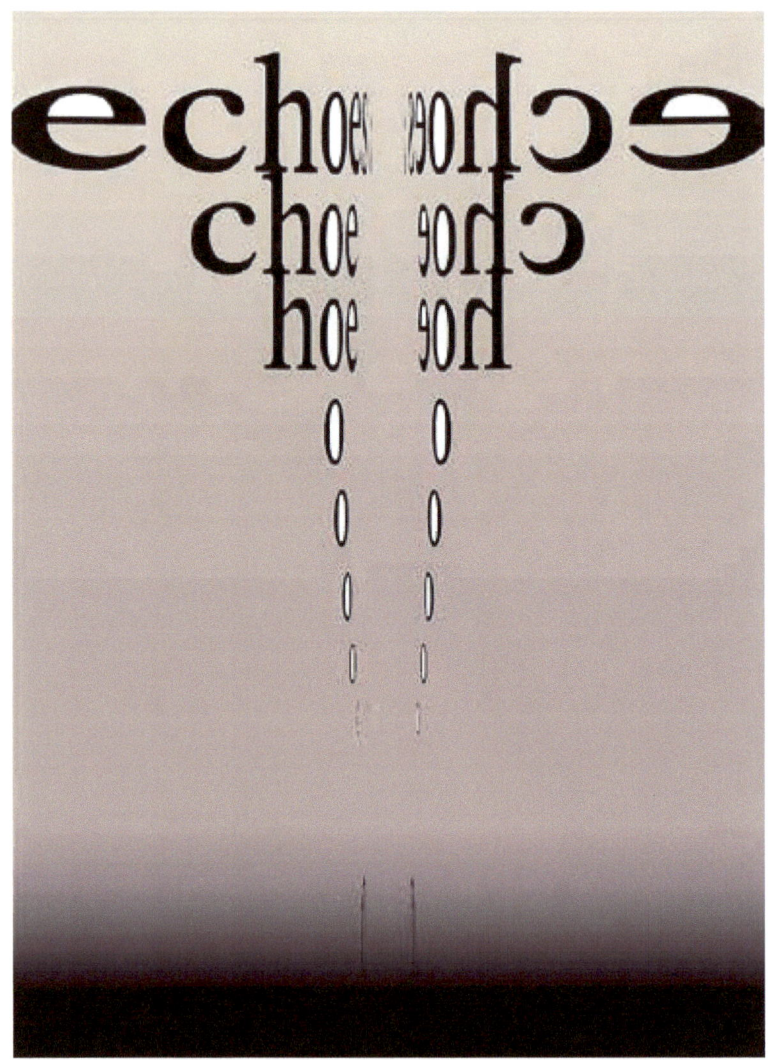
echoes
choe
hoe
o
o
o
o

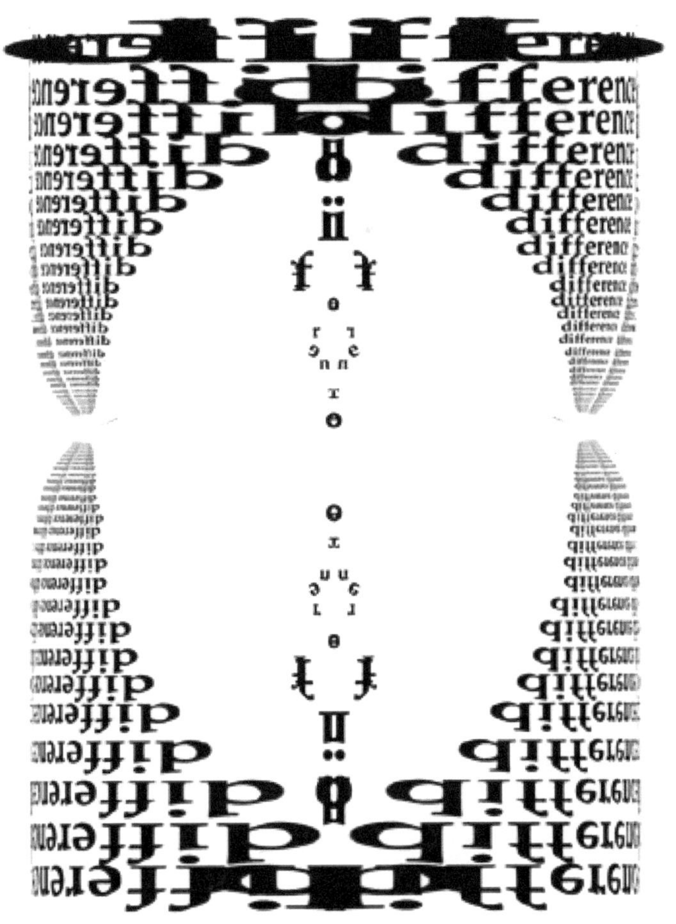

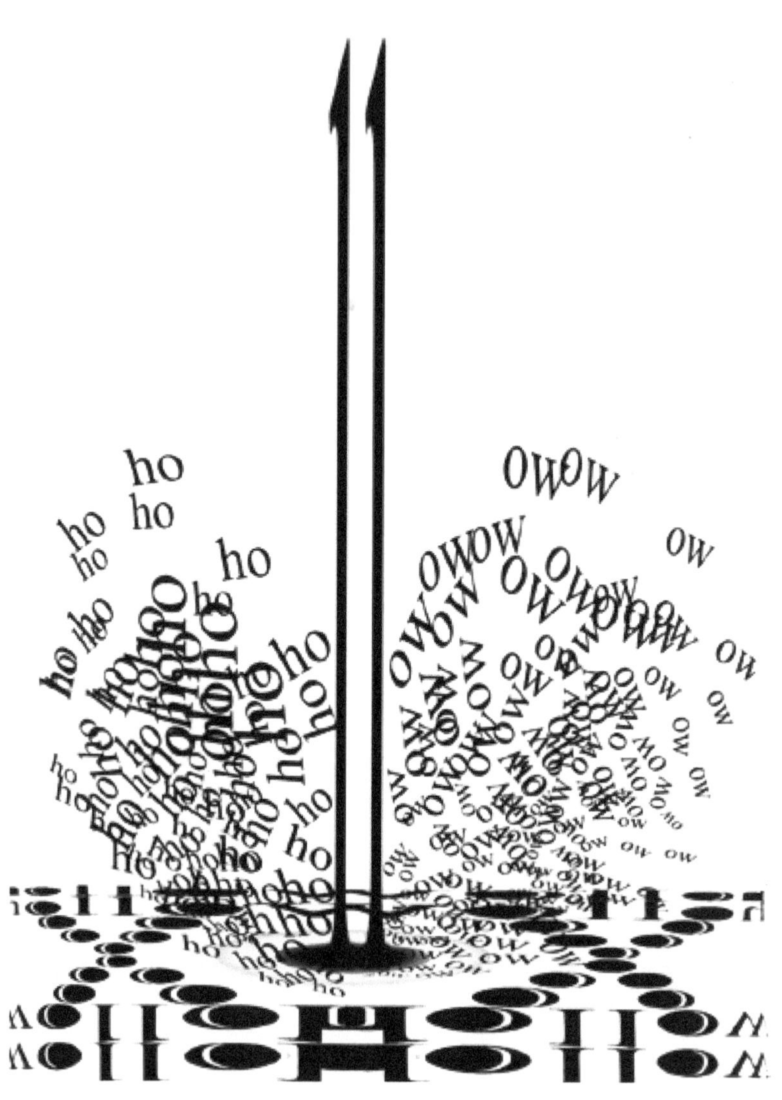

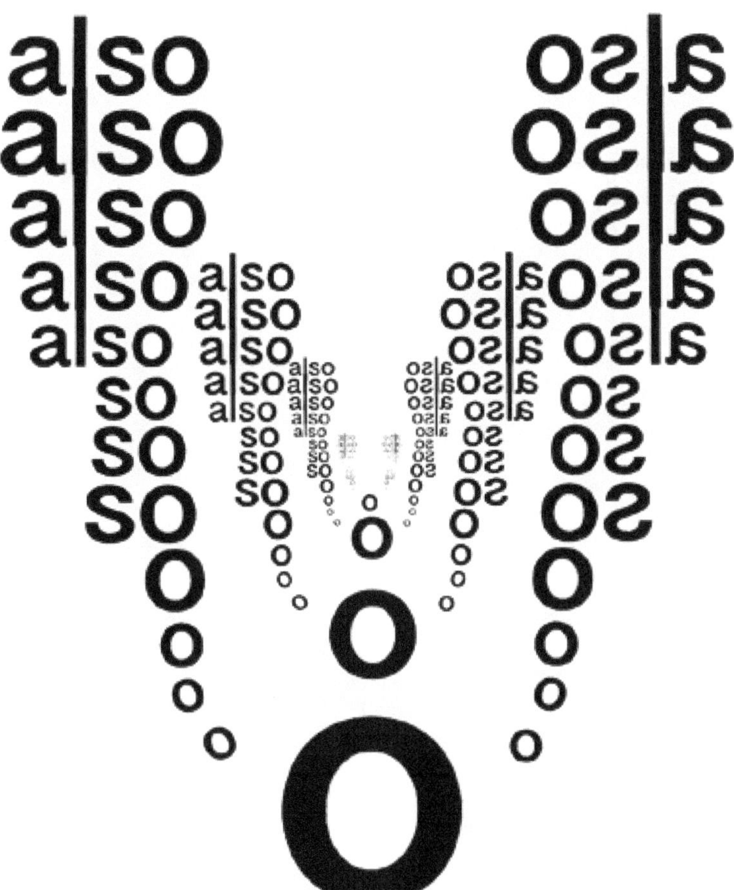

move remov
mover emov
movere mov
mover emov
move remov
move remov
mover emov
movere mov
mover emov
move remov

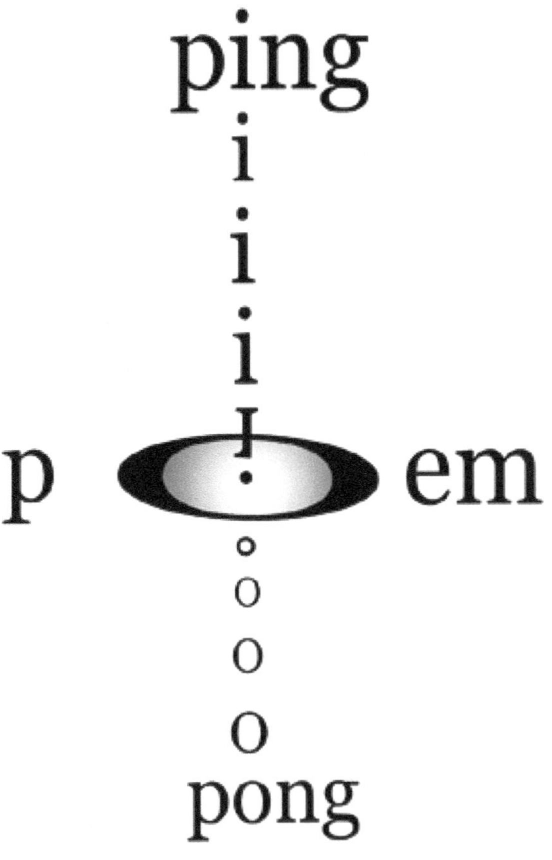
ping
i
i
i
p
em
o
o
o
pong

worte worte worte
or or or
te te te
or or or
worte worte worte
or or or
worte worte worte
or or or
te te te
or or or
worte worte worte

disappearance

disappearance

disappearance

disappearance

disappearance

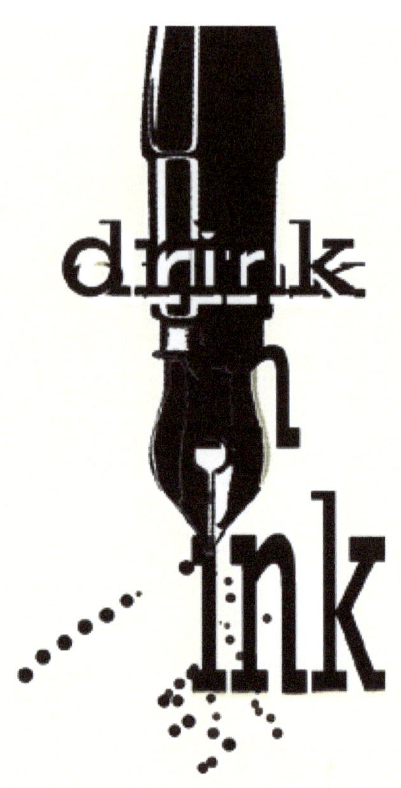
drink
ink

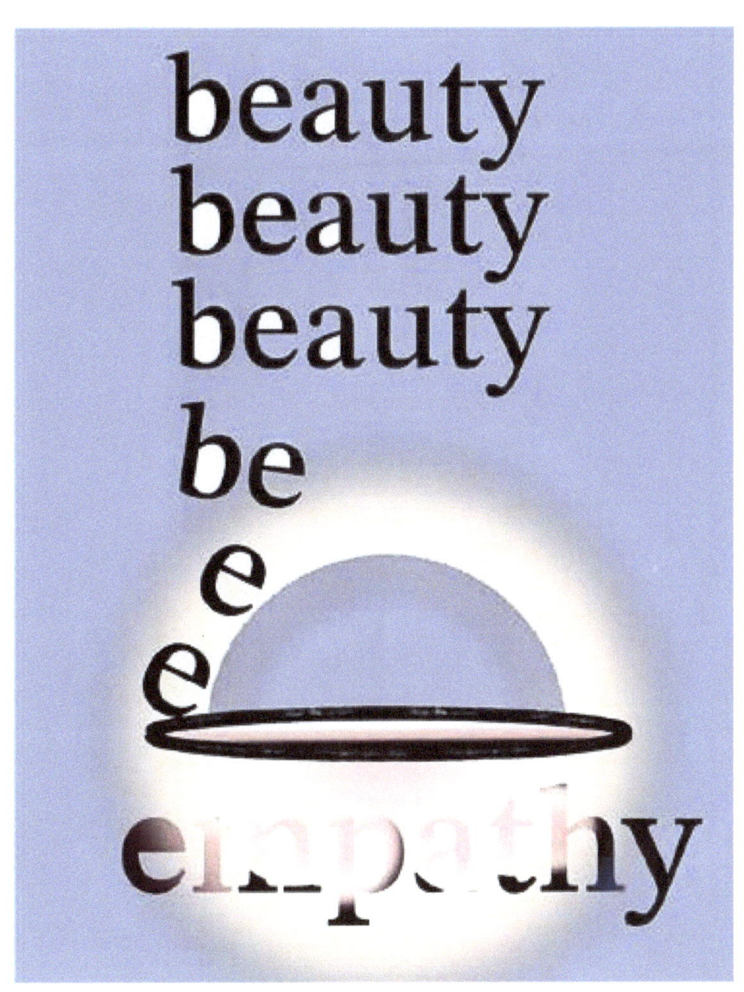
beauty
beauty
beauty
be
e
e

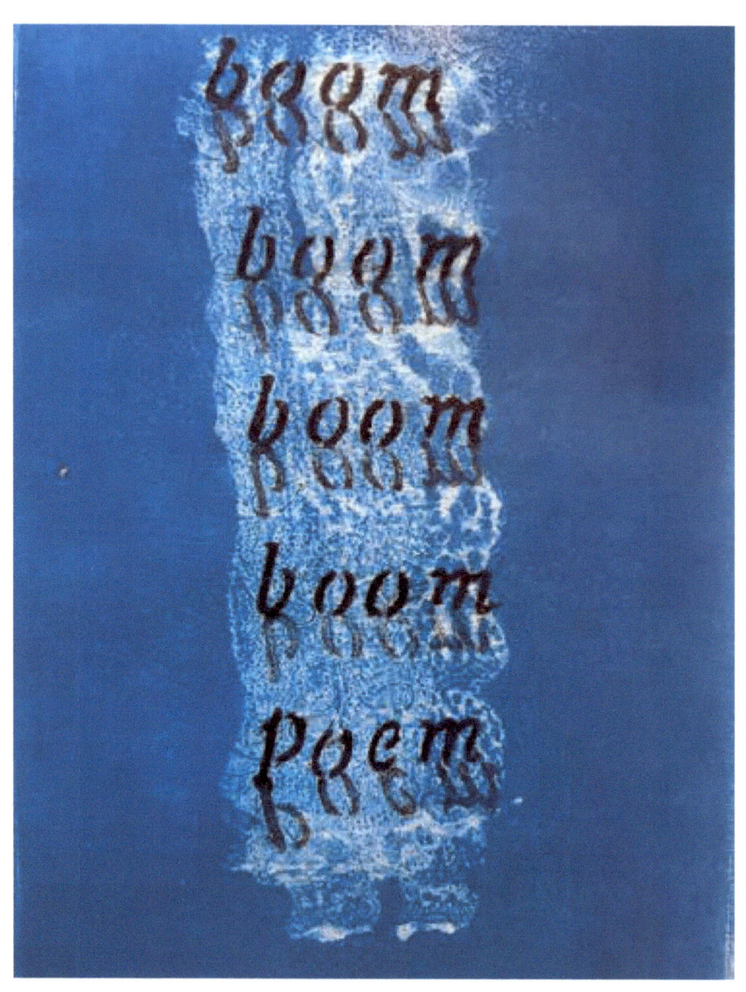

Boom Poem
Poem Boom
Boom Poem
Poem Boom

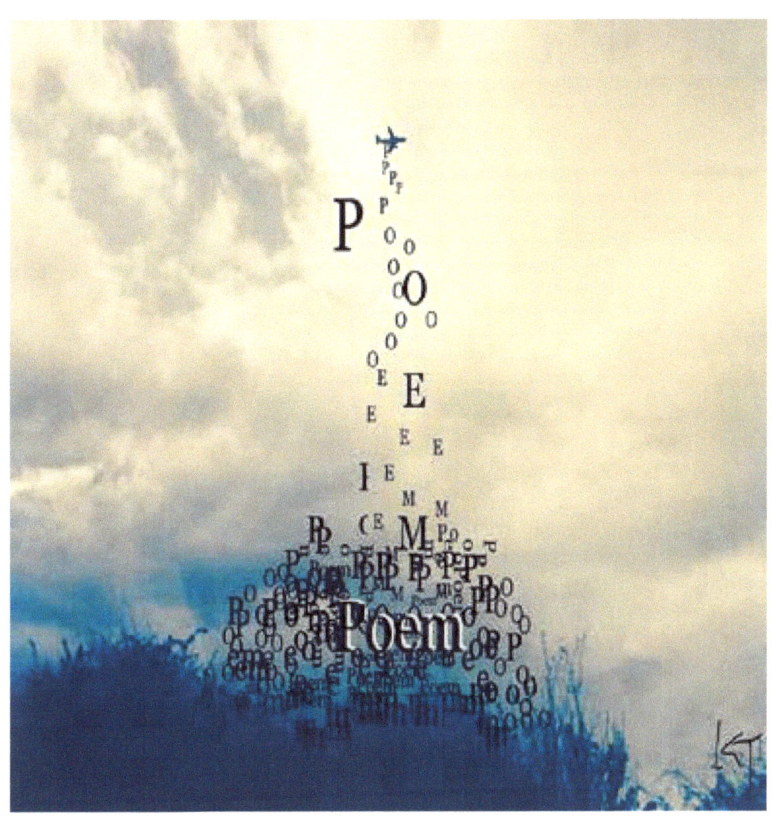

No Bomb, But Poem I

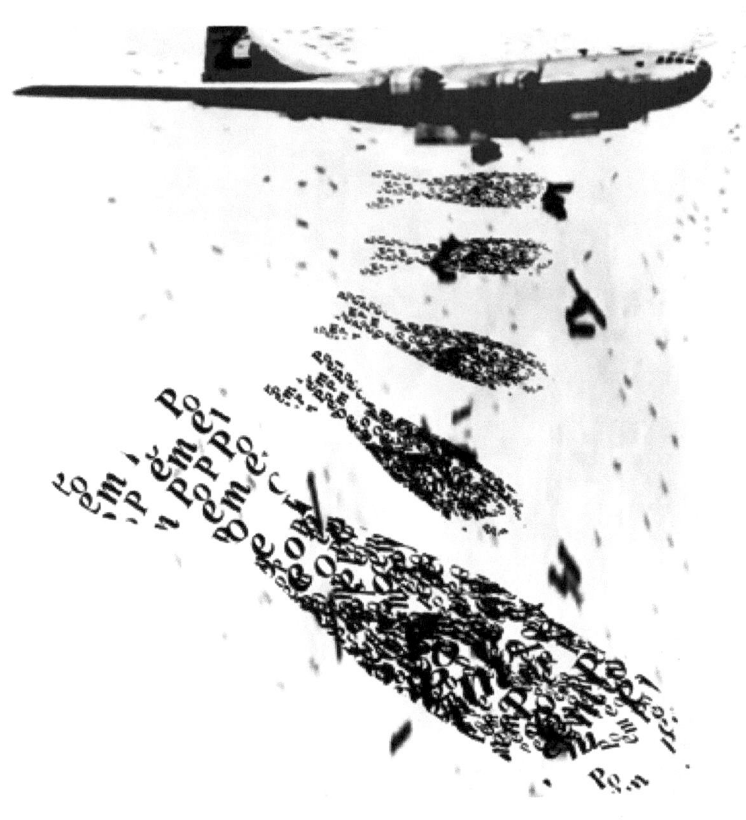

No Bomb, But Poem II

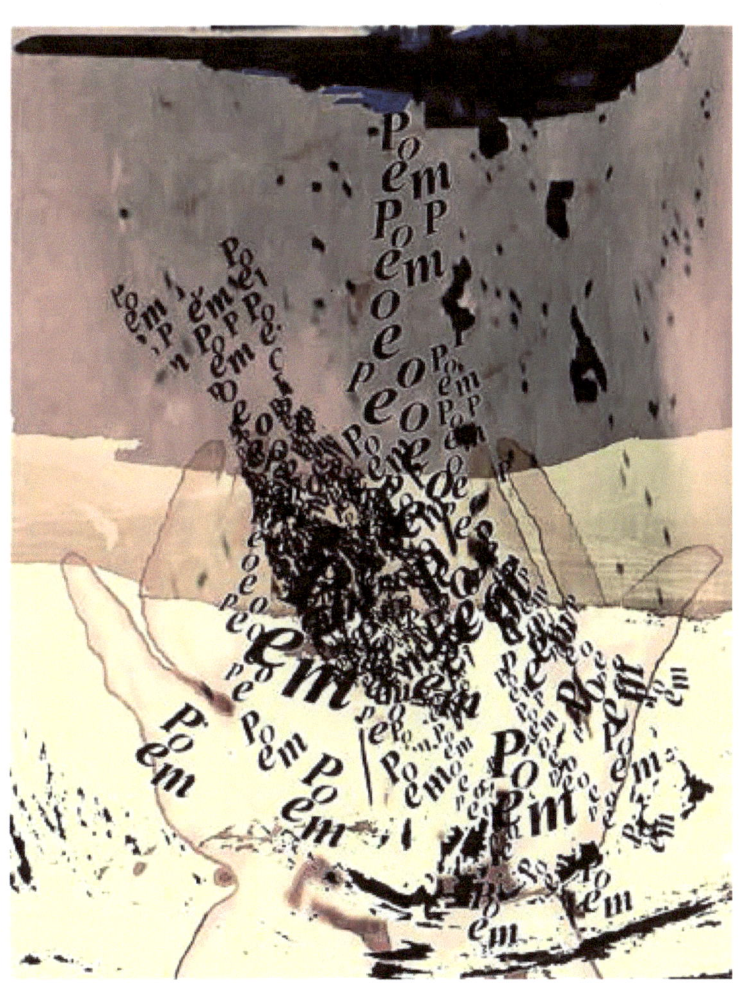

No Bomb, But Poem III

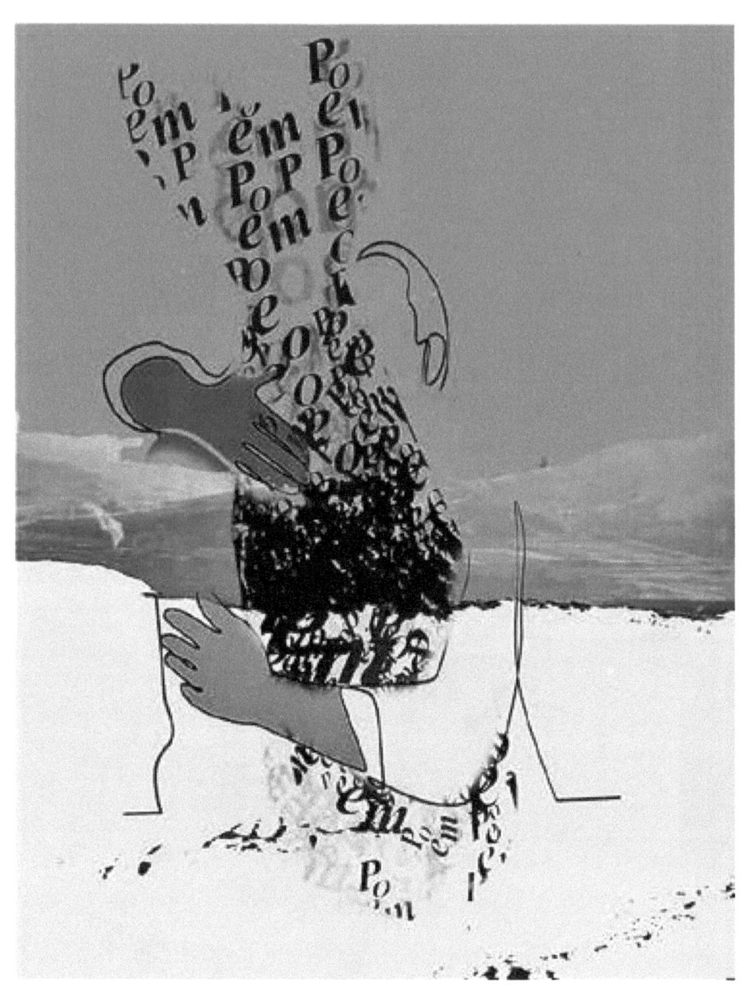

No Bomb, But Poem IV

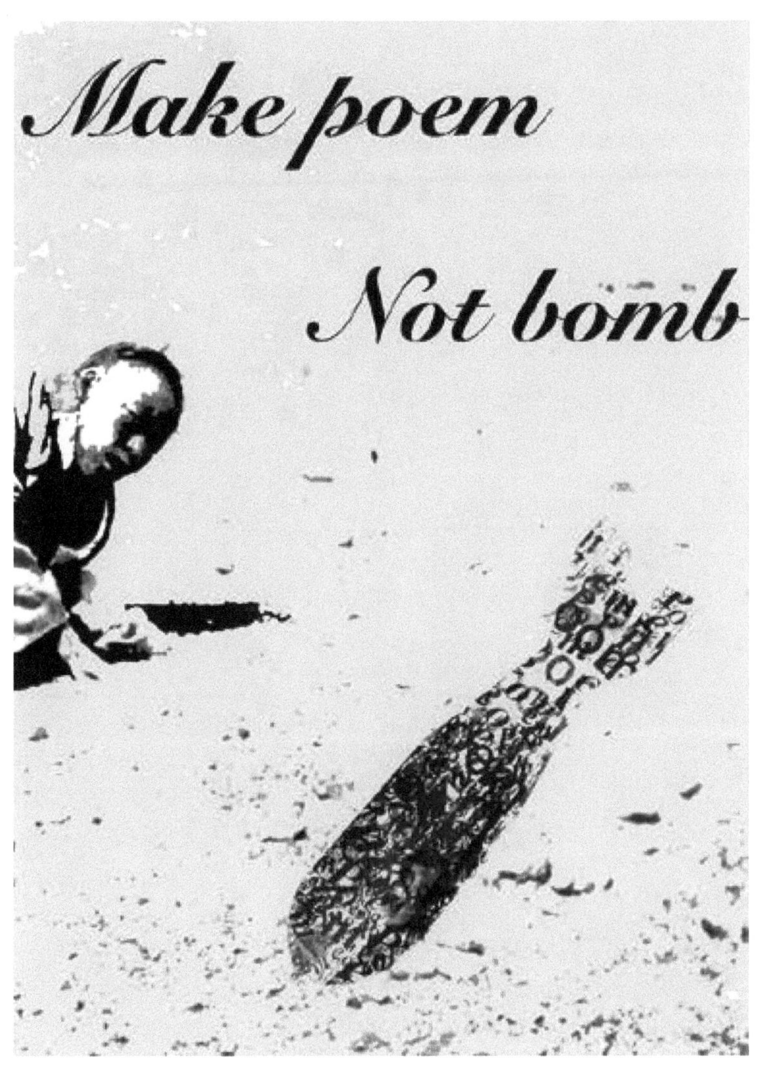

No Bomb, But Poem V

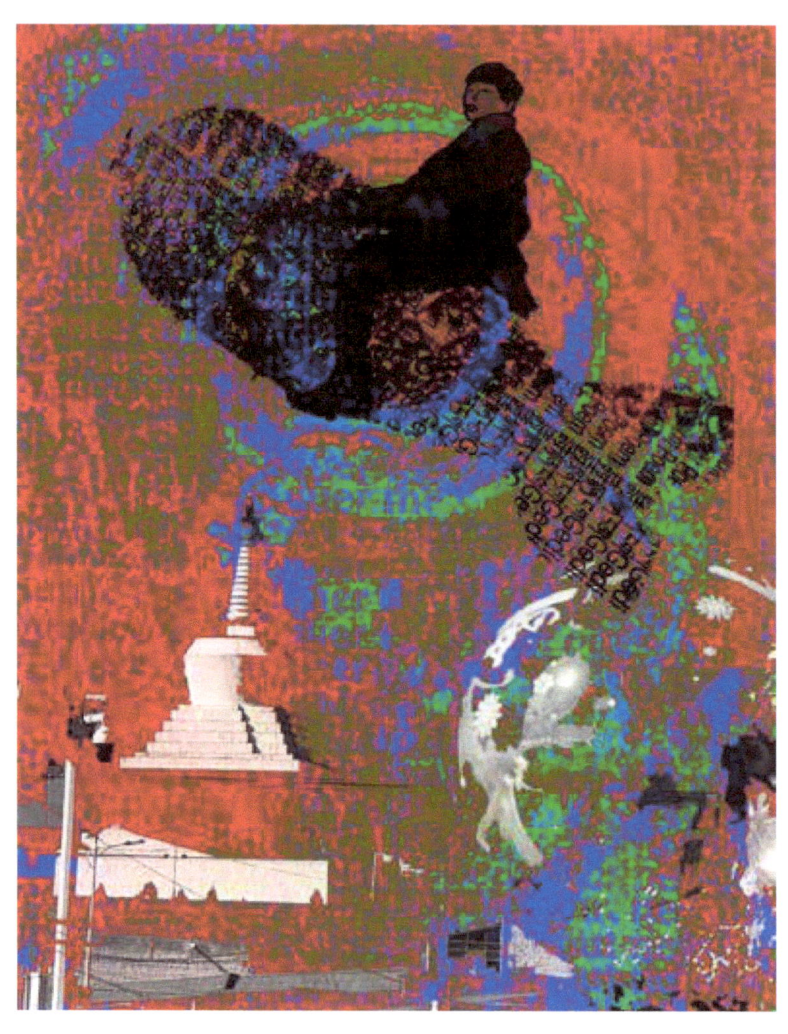

No Bomb, But Poem VI

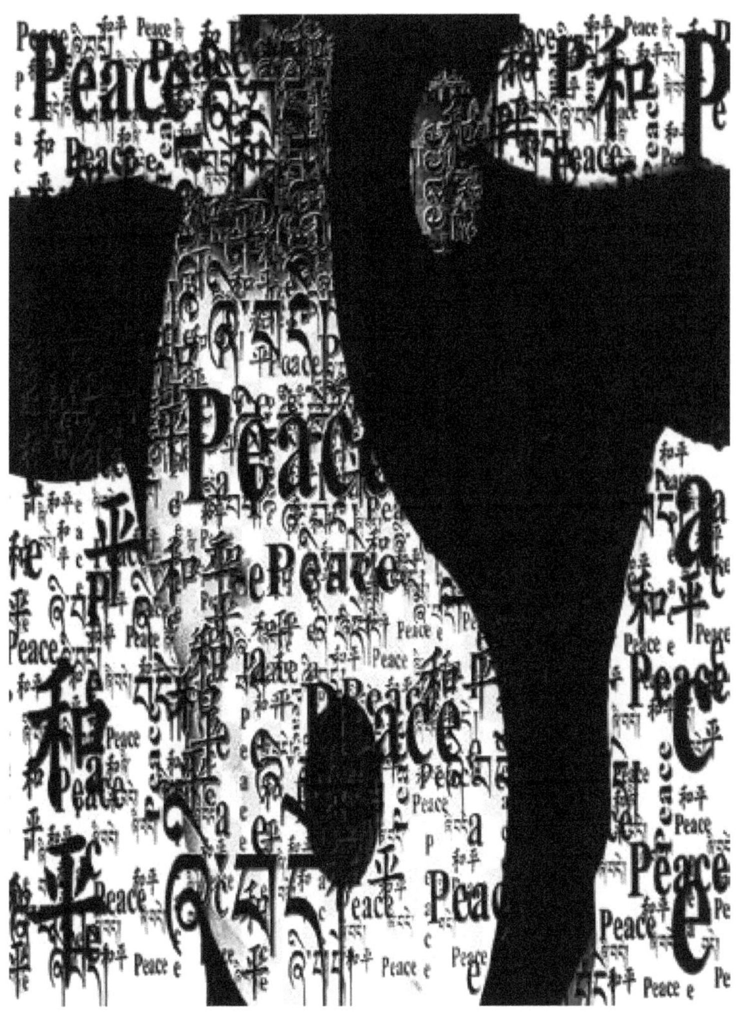

Peace

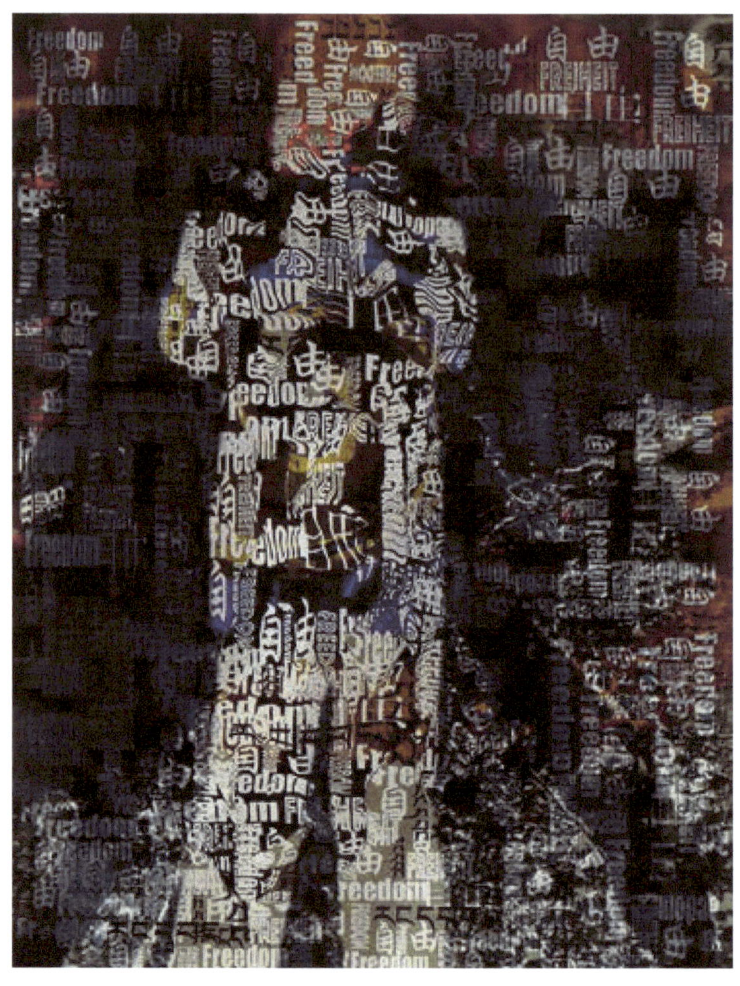

Freedom

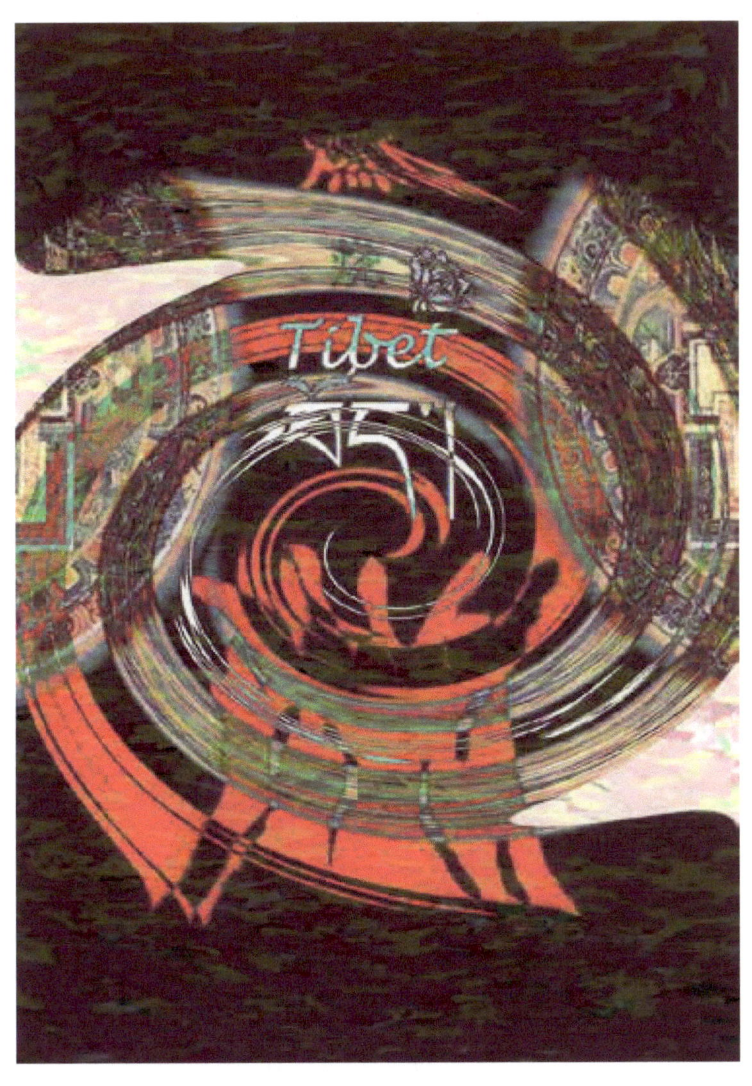

Mandala Poem I

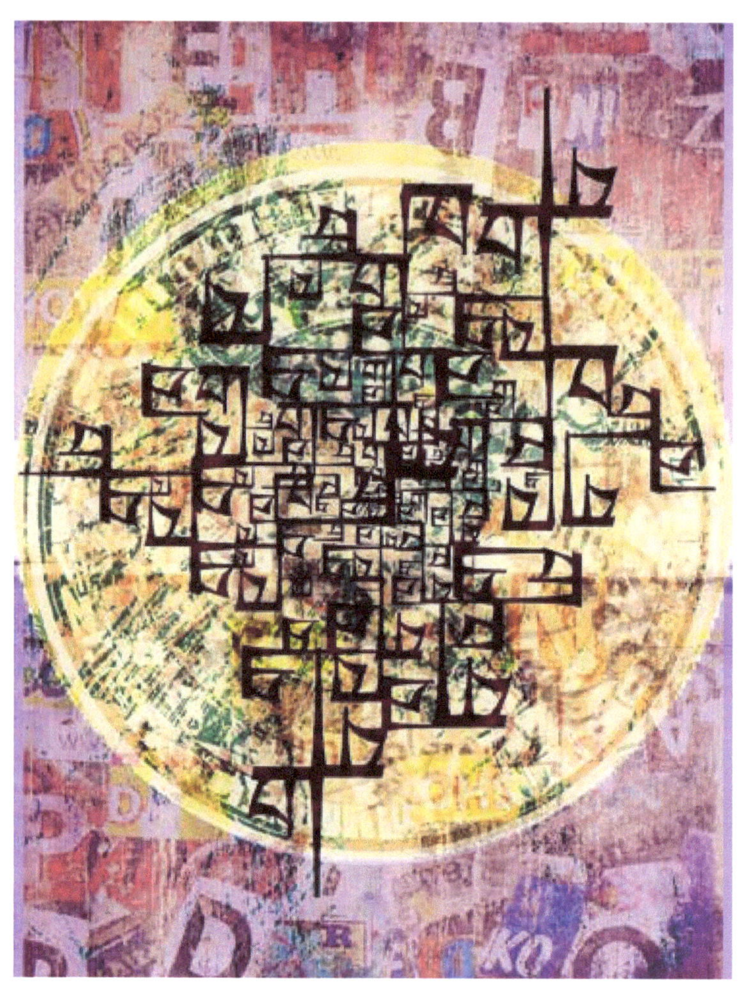

Mandala Poem II

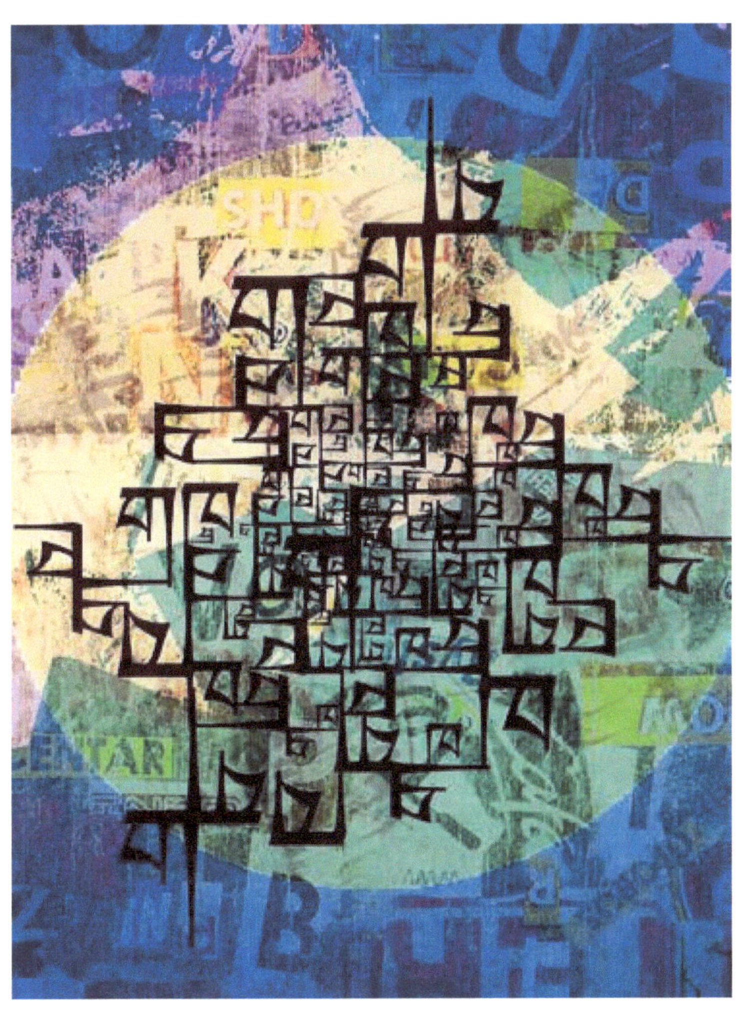

Mandala Poem III

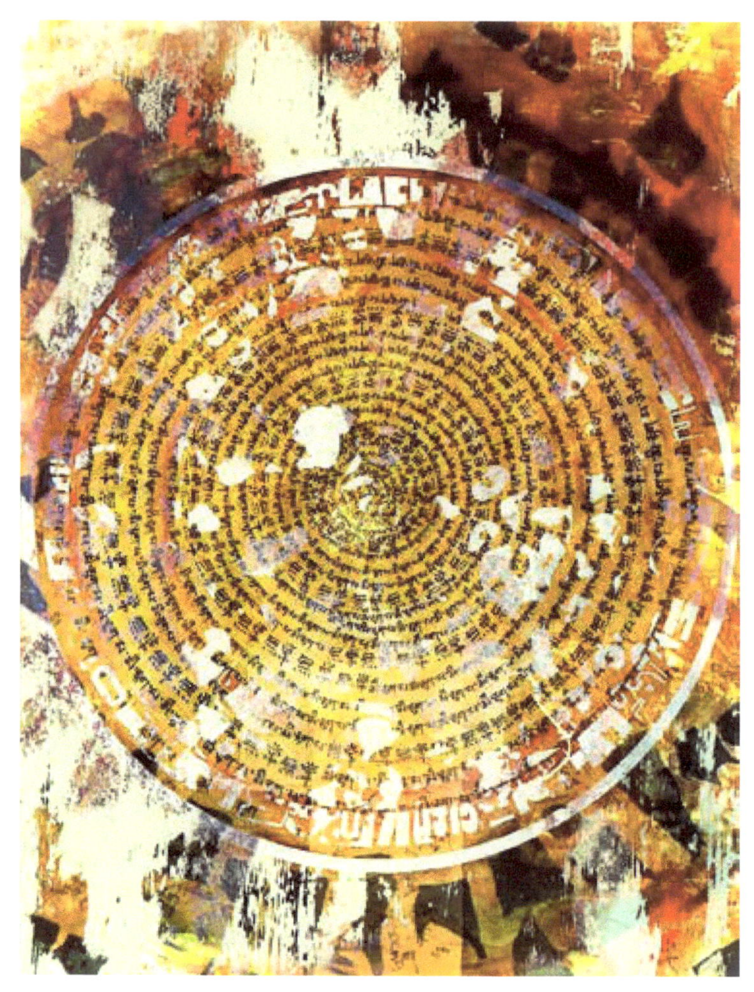

Mandala Poem IV

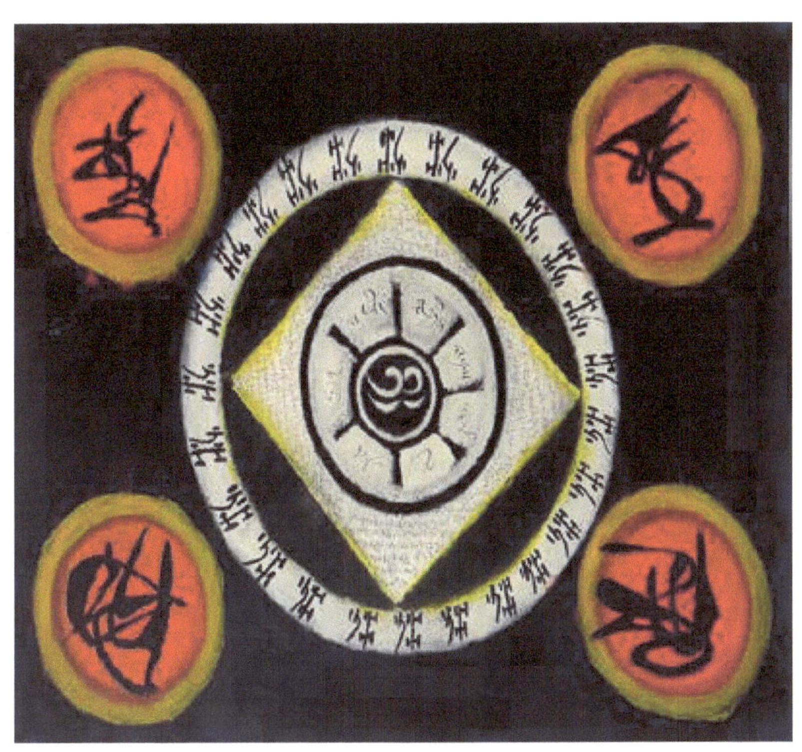

Mandala Poem V

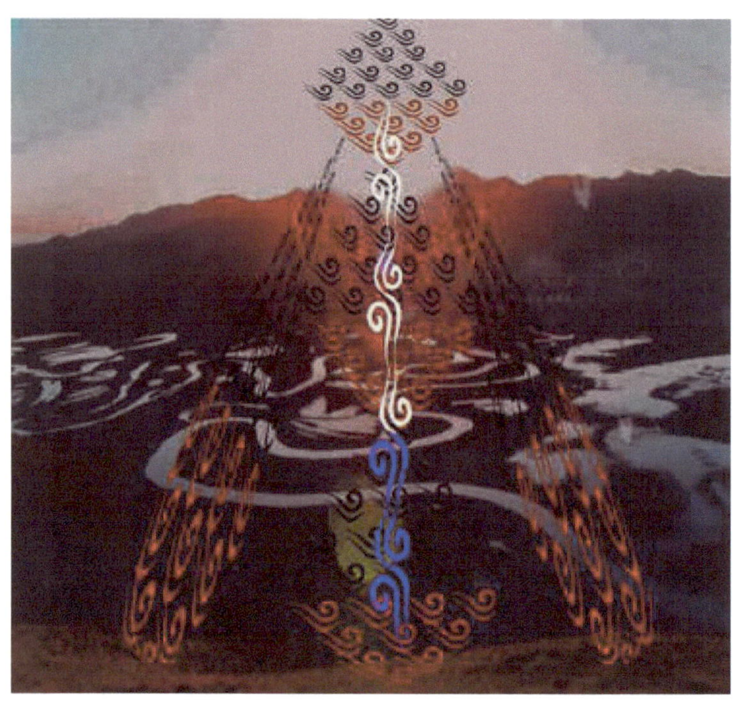

Wordless Poem

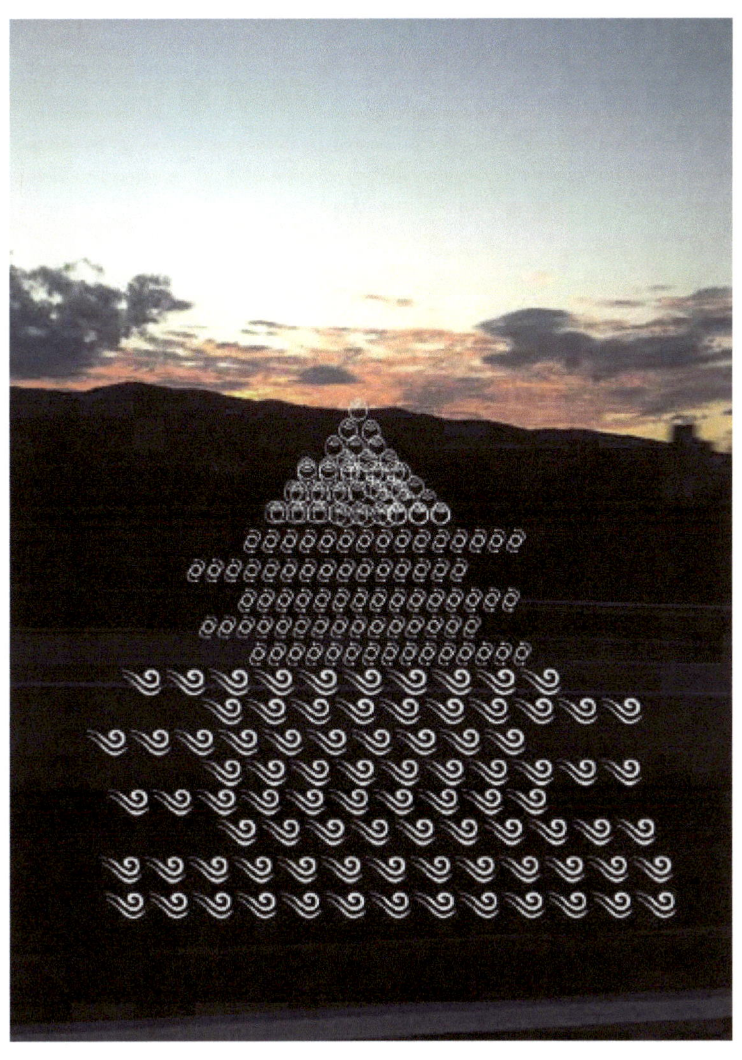

Wordless Poem II

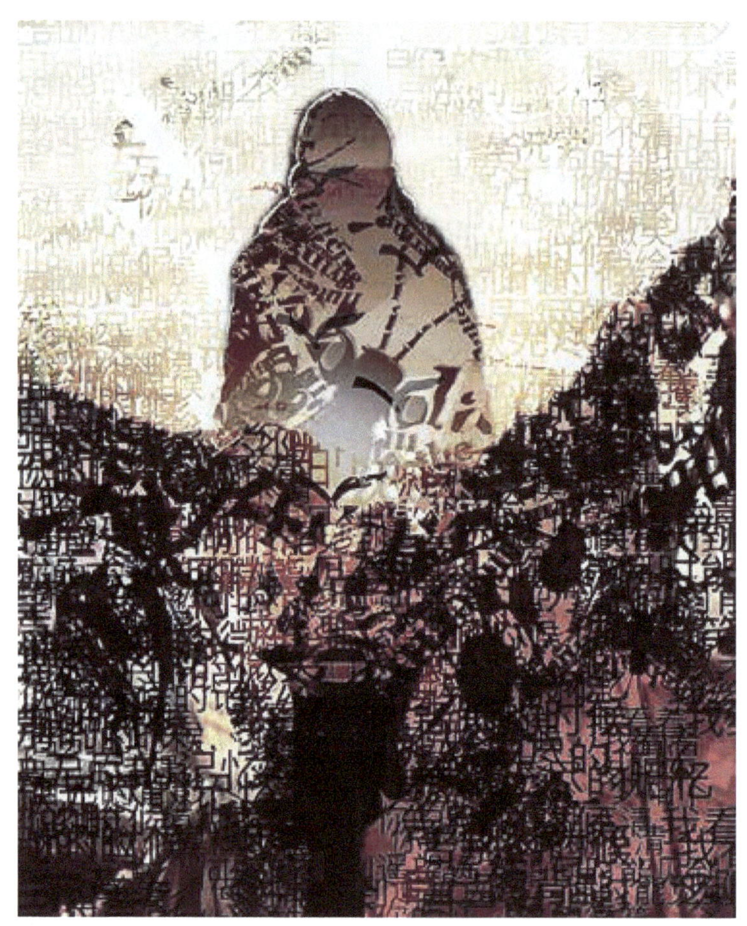

Untitled

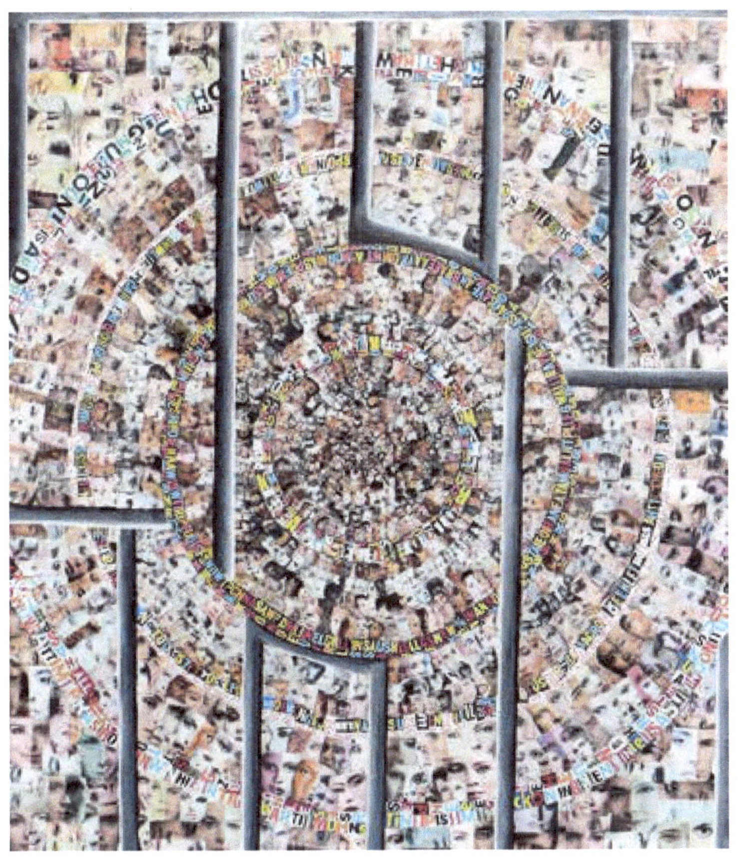

Collage I

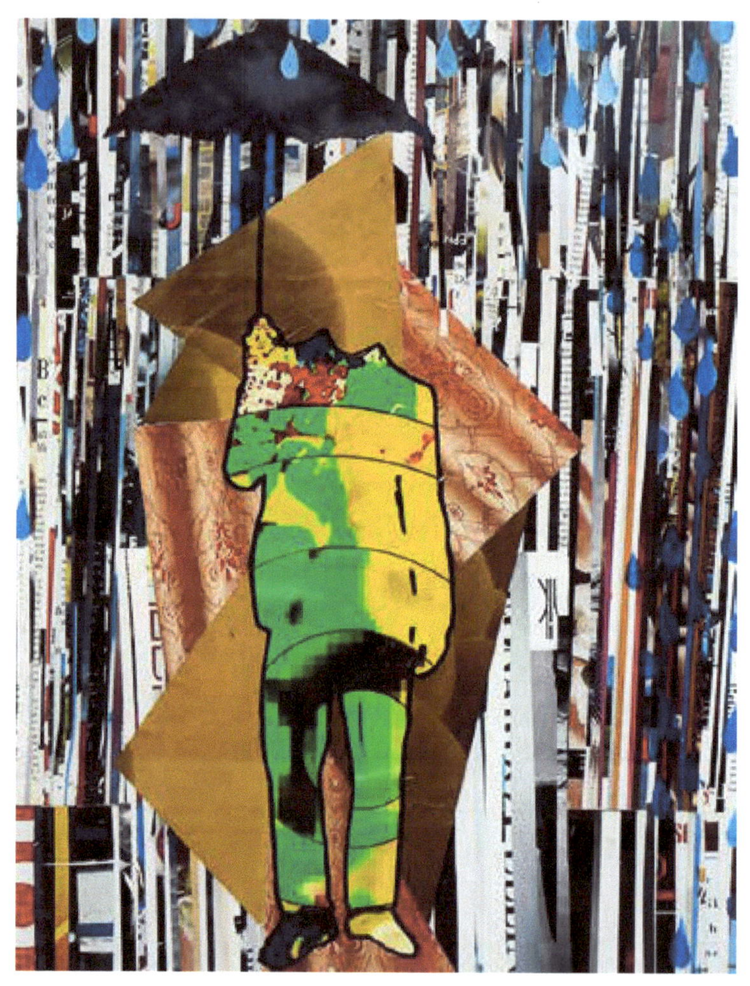

Collage II

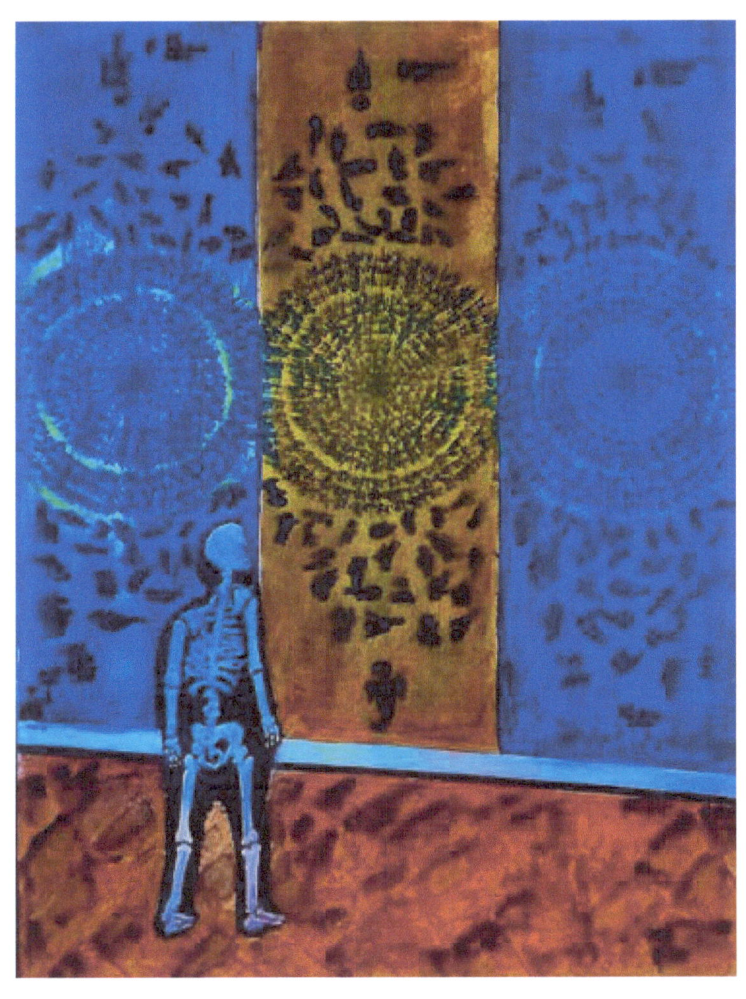

Exhibition

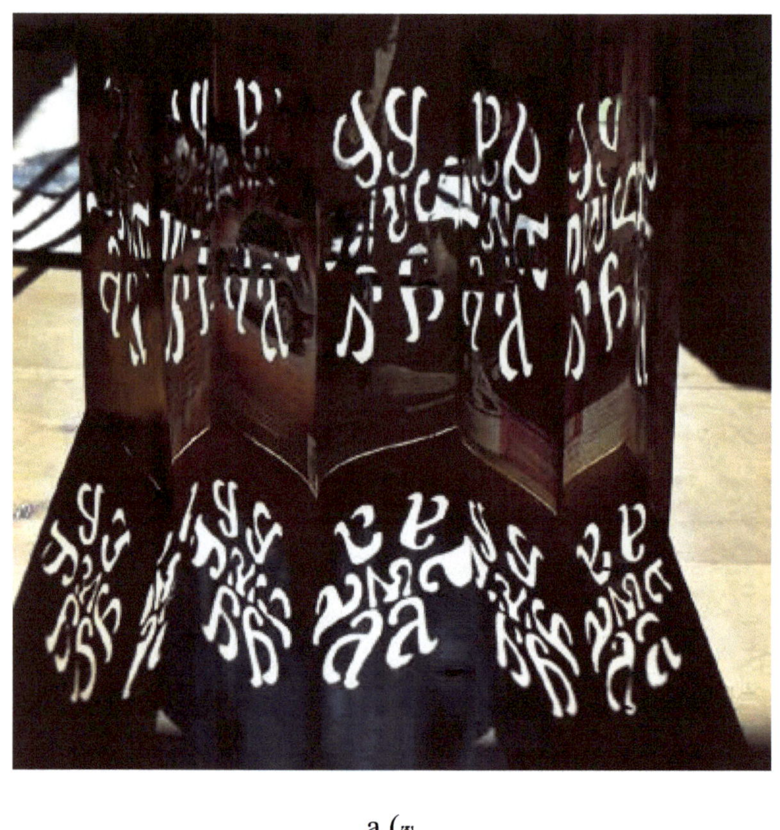

a (অ

অ)a

a (অ

অ)a

a (অ

অ)a

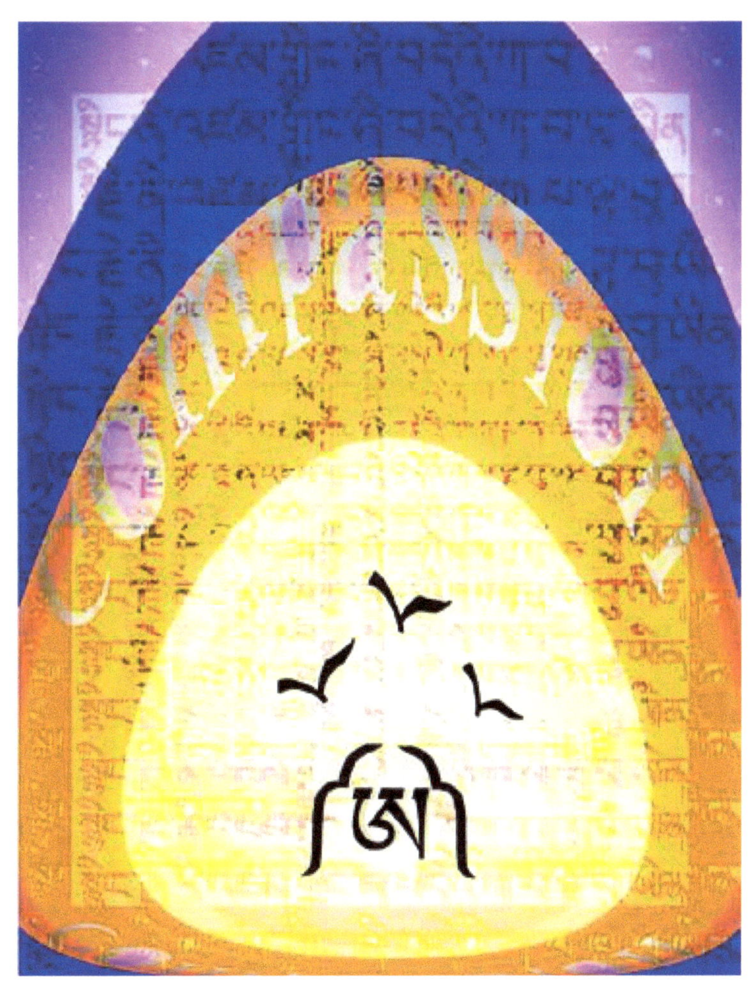

Yakman K Tsering is Tibet-born Austrian Visual Poet and artist.

His artworks have been inspired by his continual personal search into the meaning behind visual expression.

His works convey a common clarity of feeling far beyond linguistic borders and he believes visual art globalises the expression and communication.

His artworks are published in *Otoliths, E. ratio, levurlitteraire, Utsanga, Aurapoesiavisual, Mechak Center for contemporary Tibet art. Artishtonish* contemporary art magazine, and in journals in North America, Europe and Asia.

He lives and works in Austria and Germany.

www.ingramcontent.com/pod-product-compliance
Lightning Source LLC
LaVergne TN
LVHW052305100826
845147LV00006B/681